Rethinking WIC

An Evaluation of the Women, Infants, and Children Program

**Douglas J. Besharov
and
Peter Germanis**

The AEI Press

Publisher for the American Enterprise Institute
WASHINGTON, D.C.
2001

Available in the United States from the AEI Press, c/o Publisher Resources Inc., 1224 Heil Quaker Blvd., P.O. Box 7001, La Vergne, TN 37086-7001. To order, call toll free: 1-800-937-5557. Distributed outside the United States by arrangement with Eurospan, 3 Henrietta Street, London WC2E 8LU, England.

Library of Congress Cataloging-in-Publication Data

Besharov, Douglas J.
    Rethinking WIC: an evaluation of the Women, Infants, and Children Program / Douglas J. Besharov and Peter Germanis.
      p. cm.
    Includes bibliographical references and index.
    ISBN 0-8447-4148-5 (cloth: alk. paper)—ISBN 0-8447-4149-3 (pbk.: alk. paper)
      1. Special Supplemental Food Program for Women, Infants, and Children (U.S.) 2. Food relief—United States. 3. Children—United States—Nutrition. I. Germanis, Peter. II. Title.

HV696.F6 B475 2000
363.8′83′0973—dc21

1 3 5 7 9 10 8 6 4 2

The AEI Press
Publisher for the American Enterprise Institute
1150 17th Street, N.W.
Washington, D.C. 20036

Printed in the United States of America

Contents

Foreword

The AEI Evaluative Studies series consists of detailed empirical analyses of government programs and policies in action. Each study documents the history, purposes, operations, and political underpinnings of the program in question; analyzes its costs, consequences, and efficacy in achieving its goals; and presents proposals for reform. The studies are prepared by leading academic scholars in individual policy fields and are reviewed by other scholars, agency officials, and program proponents and critics before publication.

The growth of public policy research in recent decades has been accompanied by a burgeoning of research and writing on *proposed* policies and those in the initial stages of implementation. Careful evaluation of the large base of *existing* programs and policies—many of them politically entrenched and no longer at the forefront of policy debate—has suffered from relative neglect. Within the government, program evaluation is typically limited to scrutiny of annual spending levels and of the number and composition of constituents who are served. Insufficient attention is devoted to fundamental questions: whether a program's social or economic goals are being accomplished, whether the goals are worthy and important, and whether they might be better achieved through alternative approaches.

The AEI series, directed by Marvin H. Kosters, aims to redress that imbalance. By examining government programs in action, it aims to direct more academic, political, and public attention to whether we are getting our money's worth from well-established programs and whether current "policy reform" agendas are indeed focused on issues with the greatest potential for improved public welfare.

CHRISTOPHER DEMUTH
PRESIDENT
AMERICAN ENTERPRISE INSTITUTE
FOR PUBLIC POLICY RESEARCH

PART ONE

Rethinking WIC

1
Introduction

"WIC works, perhaps better than any other government program in existence," former Agriculture Secretary Dan Glickman declared.[1] Former Health and Human Services Secretary Louis Sullivan made a similar claim: "The WIC Program results in significant Medicaid savings that far outweigh the program's costs by a ratio of 3 to 1. . . . That is clearly an overwhelming return on a small national investment."[2] Such statements testify to the extraordinary bipartisan support enjoyed by WIC, the Special Supplemental Nutrition Program for Women, Infants, and Children.

Congress established WIC in 1972 as a two-year pilot program partially in response to the 1969 White House Conference on Food, Nutrition, and Health. The conference report concluded that nutritional deficiencies among low-income women and children threatened their health and led to higher medical costs.[3] To avoid preventable physical or medical conditions, WIC seeks to improve the diets and, therefore, the health of low-income pregnant, breastfeeding, and postpartum women as well as their infants and children up to age five.

Current WIC regulations, tracking the underlying legislation, describe the "general purpose and scope" of the WIC program as follows:

> Section 17 of the Child Nutrition Act of 1966, as amended, states in part that the Congress finds that substantial numbers of pregnant, postpartum, and breastfeeding women, infants and young children from families with inadequate income are at special risk with respect to their physical and mental health by reason of inadequate nutrition or health care, or both. The purpose of the Program is to provide supplemental foods and nutrition education through

3

payment of cash grants to State agencies which administer the Program through local agencies at no cost to eligible persons. The Program shall serve as an adjunct to good health care during critical times of growth and development, in order to prevent the occurrence of health problems, including drug and other harmful substance abuse, and to improve the health status of these persons.[4]

Among the conditions WIC is intended to ameliorate are prematurity and low birthweight among pregnant women and compromised development among infants and children. Peter H. Rossi explained:

The main rationale for the WIC program is that significant numbers of poor pregnant and postpartum women, infants, and children have nutritional deficiencies that endanger the proper development of fetuses, infants, or children, leading to conditions such as prematurity, neonate mortality, low birthweight, slow development, and anemia.[5]

Currently, WIC is a $5.4 billion per year program and serves about 7.3 million women and children. Although WIC is a program of the U.S. Department of Agriculture, most of its grantees are state health departments. Those state agencies, in turn, fund WIC services though local health-related agencies such as health departments, hospitals, public health clinics, and community health centers.

WIC's popularity stems from the widespread belief that research studies have proved that WIC "works." Although some studies suggest real improvements in the diets and health of recipients, the extensive benefits cited by Glickman and Sullivan relate only to research conducted on WIC's prenatal program (which involves only about 12 percent of program participants). Even there, the evidence suggests that WIC's benefits are modest at best.

Some observers argue that the exaggeration is for a good cause: It helps support the allocation of $5.4 billion a year in additional food, nutrition education, and counseling services for low-income infants and children, pregnant women, and breastfeeding or postpartum mothers. But overstating WIC's effectiveness undermines support for the research and programmatic flexibility needed to increase the program's beneficial impact. For example, over the past decade, additions to WIC's funding have had the effect of expanding the program into the lower middle class—when the increases probably could have been much more effectively used to improve or intensify services for generally needier families (a point to which we return later). WIC's rigid spending rules, for example, effectively prevent local programs from spending more than about thirty minutes for nutrition education every six months with clients and preclude enriching food packages with such items as iron supplements.

The need to improve the WIC program is crucial. Even if WIC were as effective as its advocates claim, the program must do much more to improve diet-related health outcomes for low-income Americans. In 1998 America's infant mortality rate was .7 percent of live births, or about 28,000 babies. The low-birthweight rate was about 7.6 percent of live births (up 12 percent since 1986), or about 300,000 babies.[6] Surely, we should strive for a WIC program that is as effective as possible.

Moreover, Congress developed WIC almost thirty years ago, when hunger was the major nutrition-related problem facing disadvantaged Americans. Since then, overweight has superseded hunger as our most serious nutrition-related health problem. We must now consider updating WIC's mission by adding a specific focus on preventing overweight.

Key Points

In the following pages we describe in detail the major WIC evaluations and the reasons why they show little about the program's effectiveness. On the basis of not just this body of research, but also of what we know about the impact of similar programs, we draw seven conclusions.

• Studies of WIC's impact are almost entirely nonexperimental; in other words, they are based on statistical comparisons made between those who received WIC benefits and those who did not. As a result, many are subject to severe problems of selection and simultaneity bias. Moreover, most studies are of limited applicability to assessing the current program because they are based on the program as it existed more than a decade ago and thus do not reflect the composition of the caseload today.

• WIC probably makes at least a small improvement in the diets and behaviors of some pregnant women, especially the most disadvantaged; that improvement, in turn, may improve the birth outcomes for some infants.

• WIC probably increases the nutritional intake of some infants, especially those who would not have been breastfed, but the health consequences of the increases are not clear. Moreover, WIC may reduce breastfeeding, which can have negative health consequences.

• In all, WIC probably makes little significant difference in the diets of one- to four-year-old children, but it may affect some subgroups more noticeably, especially those comprising children whose intake of nutrients one might otherwise consider inadequate.

• WIC has expanded beyond the truly disadvantaged, even though new participants are unlikely to need or benefit from the services it provides.

• WIC is largely irrelevant to the most serious nutritional problem facing disadvantaged Americans: overweight.

• WIC does not result in the major cost savings that its advocates claim, and it may not even pass a basic benefit-cost test.

As those points suggest, existing WIC research, at least when read in the most favorable light, provides some (and perhaps substantial) support for the proposition that WIC has significant social and policy effects on particular subgroups of participants. The research has not clearly established the makeup or identity of those subgroups, but they seem to comprise the neediest families—the poorest of the poor.

In the future, policymakers should pay much greater attention to such differential effects, especially because they might suggest more focused service strategies. As Peter H. Rossi noted in *Feeding the Poor: Assessing Federal Food Aid,* that lack of focus on subgroups is one of the shortcomings of most current research: "[C]urrently available evaluation studies place too much emphasis on central tendencies—means and medians—and do not give enough attention to measures of the distributions of responses and differentials among subgroups."[7]

To increase WIC's positive impacts, we propose a series of possible reforms, each to be thoroughly evaluated. To emphasize the tentative nature of our recommendations, we state them in the form of questions. Should we target WIC benefits to more needful families? Should we selectively intensify WIC benefits? Should we add a focus on preventing overweight? Should we serve children over age four? Should we increase directive counseling? Should we use alternative service providers?

Reforms along those lines have a good chance of making WIC more effective. Even if they do not, that does not mean that such expansions of the program are not socially worthwhile, *so long as they are more carefully targeted than current services.* Making even a small number of children, especially poor children, healthier—without harming others and without exorbitant spending—would be an ethical benefit not captured in purely economic benefit-cost calculations. As Jane Huntington and Frederick A. Connell wrote in the *New England Journal of Medicine:*

> [W]e should consider whether cost savings is the appropriate criterion by which to judge prenatal care programs. It is tempting to assume that in order for these programs to be valuable, they really should save more than they cost. Yet when we require prenatal care, and other preventive health care, to pay for itself, we may be inadvertently denying valuable benefits to society. It may be better to ask not "How much does this save?" but, rather, "How much is this worth?"[8]

Hence, this volume does not argue that WIC's weaknesses justify abandoning or even cutting the program. On the contrary, we argue that policymakers should undertake a sustained effort to make the program more effective. Of special importance is the need to add to WIC's objectives the reduction of overweight among disadvantaged Americans—a worsening problem that is now all but ignored. Congress should begin that effort by debating the role and impact of WIC and by granting greater flexibility to state and local WIC agencies to open the program to innovation and experimentation. In addition, as we describe in our conclusions, policymakers should carefully evaluate any changes. Furthermore, even in the absence of a waiver-based experimental strategy, the federal government should conduct a series of randomized demonstrations to determine more definitively the impact of each of WIC's program components—with particular attention paid to key subgroups. If evaluations prove those ideas sound, the result could be a major shift in who gets served and how. But that consideration should not prevent needed reform.

Chapters 2 and 3 of this volume describe the WIC program. Chapters 4, 5, and 6 review and assess the research on the program's impact. Chapter 7 recommends state-based experimentation along the lines of the policy reforms listed above. Chapter 8 calls for a series of randomized experiments to evaluate the program and any changes made to it, and chapter 9 briefly presents our conclusions. The essential descriptive points made in part 1 of this volume appear in table 1-1.

Part 2 of this volume includes comments on our study by five leading experts of WIC program research. Michael J. Brien of the University of Virginia and Christopher A. Swann of the State University of New York at Stony Brook describe their efforts to address the selection-bias problem and the implications of their findings for program targeting and

Table 1-1 WIC at a Glance

Target Group	Commonly Reported Nutritional Risks[a]	Benefits[b]	Coverage[c]	Funding FY 1999[d]	Range of Evaluation Findings[e]
Pregnant women	General obstetrical risks, inappropriate growth or weight-gain pattern, pre-pregnancy high weight for height, hematocrit or hemoglobin below state criteria, and inadequate or inappropriate nutrient intake.	**Food:** milk, eggs, iron-fortified dry cereal, vitamin C–rich juice, and dry beans or peanut butter. **Services:** nutrition education and referrals to substance-abuse counseling, OB/GYN care, family planning services, and other health and social services.	845,000 69% of eligibles 28% of pregnant women	$510 million Average food package: $38	**Average birthweight:** 0 to 4% (6% for blacks); after correcting for selection bias: –11 to 14% (for blacks only) **Low-birthweight rate:** 0 to –30% (–40% for blacks) **Very low birthweight rate:** 0 to –55% **Preterm birth rate:** 0 to –30% **Infant mortality rate:** 0 to –66% **Neonatal mortality rate:** 0 to –66% **Postneonatal mortality rate:** 0
Breastfeed-ing and postpartum women	General obstetrical risks, hematocrit or hemoglobin below state criteria, inade-quate or inappropriate nutrient intake, and high weight for height.	**Food:** cheese, milk, juice, dried beans or peas, peanut butter, canned tuna fish, and carrots. **Services:** nutrition education, breastfeeding promotion, and referrals to family planning services and other health and social services.	899,000 122% of eligibles 22% of women with infants	$490 million Average food package: $33	**Breastfeeding initiation and duration:** insufficient evidence **Postpartum women;** subsequent birthweight: 3 to 4% (1 study)
Infants (0–12 months)	Infant of a WIC-eligible mother or mother at risk during pregnancy and breastfeeding mother and infant dyad.	**Food:** concentrated, liquid, iron-fortified formula (or powdered or other formula), iron-fortified dry infant cereal, and vitamin C–rich infant juice. **Services:** referrals to pediatric care, immunization services, and other health services.	1,898,000 122% of eligibles 49% of infants	$900 million Average food package: $27 ($89 before rebate)	**Anemia:** reduction; not possible to quantify **Adequately immunized:** 0 to 36% (1 study) **Mean nutrient intake:** vitamin C (59%) and iron (32%) (1 study)

| Children (1–4 years) | Inadequate or inappropriate nutrient intake, hematocrit or hemoglobin below state criteria, and high weight for height. | **Food:** milk, eggs, iron-fortified dry cereal, vitamin C–rich juice, and dry beans or peanut butter. **Services:** nutrition education and referral to EPSDT and other health services. | 3,670,000 75% of eligibles 25% of children | $2,050 million Average food package: $34 | **Anemia:** reduction; not possible to quantify **Adequately immunized:** 0 to 25% (1 study) **Mean nutrient intake:** positive for 1/3 to 2/3 of nutrients studied, most notably iron (about 20%) (2 studies) |

a. This table reports the most commonly reported nutritional risks, affecting at least 15 percent of WIC participants in 1996 (Randall, Bartlett, and Kennedy 1998, 85).

b. Food packages are tailored to meet the individual needs of participants, so the food packages described identify the foods most commonly provided for each target group. The services provided reflect those offered in WIC clinics.

c. The percentage of eligibles was last reported for 1997 in U.S. Department of Agriculture, Food and Nutrition Service (1999). Because pregnant women are unlikely to participate in WIC for a full forty weeks, their participation rate is expected to be less than 100 percent. For example, if all eligible pregnant women enrolled in WIC for six months, their participation rate would be 65 percent. According to the USDA, the high participation rates for some groups are due to differences between the way the number of income-eligibles is estimated and the certification practices applied in local WIC agencies. In addition, some imprecision is present in any survey-based estimate. But according to the USDA report, "[T]hese data do strongly suggest that the program has likely achieved virtually full coverage of persons in this category at the national level." The percentage of the population covered was estimated by using population data from the U.S. Bureau of the Census. The number of pregnant women was estimated by assuming that they equal three-fourths of the number of infants, because pregnancy lasts nine months, while infancy lasts twelve months.

d. U.S. Department of Agriculture, Food and Nutrition Service (2000). Funding for each target group was estimated by adding the average administrative cost of $12 per participant to the average cost of food for each target group and then multiplying by the average monthly number of recipients. That is then multiplied by twelve to arrive at an annual cost.

e. Findings for birth outcomes are from Devaney, Bilheimer, and Schore (1990); Devaney (1992); Gordon and Nelson (1995); Gordon (1993); and Brien and Swann (1997, 1999b). Findings for breastfeeding women are not presented, because the only available research is not representative of the current WIC program. Findings for postpartum women are from Caan et al. (1987). Findings for infant outcomes are from Rush, Leighton, et al. (1988). Findings for children's immunization status are from Rush, Leighton, et al. (1988). Findings for children's nutrient intake were calculated by using data from Rose, Habicht, and Devaney (1998) and Oliveira and Gunderson (2000). Findings for the decline in prevalence of anemia are from Yip et al. (1987).

design. Nancy R. Burstein of Abt Associates explains the methodological problems encountered in dealing with selection bias and then describes an incremental approach to testing the efficacy of WIC with randomized experiments. Barbara Devaney of Mathematica Policy Research offers a defense of the existing research by arguing that we have overstated the research problems in assessing WIC's effectiveness. She does, however, offer support for some of the policy options we present. Robert Greenstein of the Center on Budget and Policy Priorities also argues that we have overstated the research problems affecting WIC and concludes that we are overly pessimistic about the program's impact. Like Devaney, he believes that some of the policy ideas deserve "serious consideration" but considers others to be "troubling" and likely to reduce WIC's effectiveness.

Instead of attempting to address the disagreements that exist between us and the commentators in a separate response, we have done our best to reflect the basis of our conclusions in the main text.

2

Program Benefits

WIC has three parts: vouchers to purchase specific high-nutrition food packages to supplement diets,[1] nutritional and health counseling, and referrals to health care and social service providers.

Food Packages

After applicants are approved for participation in the WIC program, they receive WIC vouchers that are valid for one to three months, after which the agency must reissue vouchers. Like food stamps, vouchers can be redeemed only at participating food stores.[2] But unlike in the case of food stamps, which enable recipients to "purchase" a wide array of foods, program participants can exchange WIC vouchers for only specified foods included in the WIC "food package." Participants cannot even exchange the vouchers for vitamins or nonfood nutritional supplements.

The amount of WIC benefits people receive is not related to their household size or income, as are food stamps and many other social programs, but rather to the age and pregnancy status of recipients. Recipients receive one of seven basic food packages, depending on each recipient's category and nutritional need.[3]

WIC's food packages are meant to supplement the diets of recipients rather than to meet their entire food needs. The foods included in the packages are high in protein, calcium, iron, and vitamins A and C and are designed to provide the nutrients often lacking in the diets of WIC's target populations. Packages typically include iron-fortified infant cereal and formula, juice, milk, cheese, eggs, peanut butter, and beans.

Many WIC agencies tailor food packages to meet the nutritional deficiencies of individual WIC clients. For example, if the agency knows
that a WIC participant has high cholesterol, the agency may modify the
standard food package to replace such high-cholesterol foods as eggs
and regular peanut butter with such low-cholesterol foods as reduced-
fat peanut butter and skim milk.

Detailed federal regulations set the content of the WIC food package
and allow relatively little flexibility for altering it. The regulations establish seven basic food packages, depending on the category and nutritional need of the recipient. U.S. Department of Agriculture regulations
precisely describe the content and amount of food in each of those packages. For example, the food package for children and women with special dietary needs (Food Package III) is described as follows:

(i) Formula intended for use as an oral feeding and prescribed by a
physician.

(ii) Cereal (hot or cold) which contains a minimum of 28 milligrams of iron per 100 grams of dry cereal and not more than 21.2
grams of sucrose and other sugars per 100 grams of dry cereal (6
grams per ounce).

(iii) Single strength fruit juice or vegetable juice, or both, which
contains a minimum of 30 milligrams of vitamin C per 100 milli-
meters; or frozen concentrated fruit or vegetable juice, or both,
which contains a minimum of 30 milligrams of vitamin C per 100
milliliters of reconstituted juice.[4]

In addition, the regulations specify monthly maximums, such as 403
fluid ounces of concentrated liquid formula, 36 ounces of dry cereal,
and 138 fluid ounces of single-strength juice.

Those are maximums, and local agencies may provide smaller
amounts. With few exceptions, however, the agencies cannot deviate
from the basic food package.[5] Nonfood nutritional supplements, even if
medically indicated, are prohibited.

In 1999 the average WIC food package was worth about $49 per
month, but the actual cost to the government was only $33 because of
manufacturers' rebates on infant formula.[6] That amount is the average
across all WIC recipients, however. The total value of the two WIC food
packages provided to a postpartum mother and her newborn can be
about $120 a month. Table 2-1 shows the average monthly cost of WIC
food packages for the program's various target groups and the actual

Table 2-1   Monthly WIC Food Package Costs, 1999

Target Group	Cost
Pregnant women	$37.59
Breastfeeding	$37.60
Postpartum	$30.16
For all women	$35.69
Infants	$26.96 ($89.19 before rebate)
Children	$34.08
Entire WIC population	$32.52 ($48.68 before rebate)

Source: U.S. Department of Agriculture, Food and Nutrition Service, Office of Analysis and Evaluation (2000, 2).

value of the infant food package, both before and after taking into account the rebates.

Many WIC recipients may not, however, consume all the foods provided in their food package. A recent report by the USDA's Center for Nutrition Policy and Promotion used data from the Third National Health and Nutrition Examination Survey 1988–1994 to assess how well WIC food packages help recipients attain a healthy diet. The study found that "WIC women of all categories demonstrate nutrition deficiencies in their diets,"[7] despite their participation in the program. In fact, for some nutrients, intake was below the level provided by the WIC package, a finding that led the researchers to conclude that the women were not consuming their full WIC food package.[8] They speculated that possible reasons for that result included "food consumption by other household members, food preferences, or lack of effective nutrition education."[9] In addition, nonbreastfeeding, postpartum women may have limited their food consumption to return to their prepregnancy weight.

A more obvious explanation may be that WIC acts more as an income supplement than a food package. Very few of the people who receive WIC have no income. Thus, economic theory suggests that WIC vouchers free up cash that program participants might otherwise have used to purchase food. So the real questions are, How much does WIC lead to additional consumption of food, and how much does WIC free up household funds for other purposes? Researchers investigating those issues with respect to the Food Stamp Program have concluded that the program is "primarily an income maintenance program and is a nutrition program to a minor degree."[10] Rossi explained that WIC may produce a similar phenomenon:

Although WIC benefits are less in dollar value and of limited duration [than food stamps], the question may be raised whether the
vouchers simply replace ordinary income resulting in no significant change in food purchasing amount or quality or whether the
vouchers significantly alter food purchases patterns in the desired
direction. Vouchers for pregnant women, for example, are nomi-
nally earmarked for milk, eggs, fortified fruit juices, and cereal.
Does this earmarking typically mean that more of these foods are
purchased and consumed? Or do the foods obtained with WIC
vouchers simply replace what would have otherwise been purchased
from ordinary income? The evidence that prenatal participation
leads to expected birth outcome benefits suggests that diet supplementation overbalances substitution effects, but direct evidence
would be more convincing.[11]

Of course, WIC benefits could serve both purposes and probably do.
Toward the end of this volume, we suggest a randomized experiment to
help tease out the relationship.

Furthermore, the misuse of WIC vouchers also seems to be a problem of undetermined size. A recent U.S. General Accounting Office study
reports that its survey of WIC directors identified nearly 3,800 vendors
(about 9 percent of the total) as having committed fraud or abuse within
a two-year period.[12] The types of activities ranged from relatively minor
infractions, such as inappropriate substitutions of food, to more serious
ones, such as exchanging food vouchers for cash.

Nutritional and Health Counseling

Each time WIC recipients are certified, they must be offered at least two
nutrition education sessions. Those are voluntary sessions that generally last about fifteen minutes; vouchers cannot be conditioned on attendance, although some participants apparently do not know that.
Agencies may offer the sessions on an individual or group basis to teach
the importance of good nutrition and its relationship to good health.
The sessions also instruct participants how to deal with their own particular nutritional risks and those of their children. Pregnant women are
encouraged to breastfeed, for example, unless doing so is not medically
advisable.

Agencies must pay for the education sessions from an amount desig-
nated for "nutrition services and administration." Besides the administrative costs of managing the program (for example, salaries and rent),

that amount must cover the actual services to families, such as nutrition assessment and certification, nutrition education, outreach, and referral to other health and social services.

The USDA limits the amount states can spend on "nutrition services and administration." In 1999 that amount was only about $12 per participant per month. The amount is based on a formula that essentially limits expenditures to an inflation-adjusted cost per participant.[13] States may vary the amount spent on individual recipients, but the total they spend must fall within the USDA limit. Local WIC agencies are required to spend at least one-sixth of their administrative funds on nutrition education.

Evidence indicates that the cap is excessively low, or at least that, under the cap, agencies are increasingly unable to provide the level of services that they once did. To assess the impact of WIC's rapid growth and new regulatory and legislative requirements imposed during the 1988 to 1993 period, researchers at Macro International and the Urban Institute conducted a mail survey of all state WIC agencies and a nationally representative sample of local agencies along with case studies in twenty-two local agencies.[14] Among the new mandates were measures encouraging cost containment, providing education on drug abuse, encouraging breastfeeding and immunizations, expanding access to homeless women, incarcerated women, and working mothers, and requiring public assistance agencies, including WIC agencies, to provide voter registration services.

Susan Miller, a trainer of nutrition educators, described the imposition of one of those requirements, the requirement that WIC offices serve as voter registration agencies, as follows:

> Adding voter registration to the "laundry lists" of things that must be covered at a first visit just about did people in. Can we do something at the national level about the number of topics that must be covered with participants, especially at the first visit? We overwhelm people with information. This runs contrary to everything we know and preach about educating adult learners. Perhaps we could develop some options/flexibility on how to deliver information and could be less stringent in our demands on what is covered at that first visit.[15]

Macro International and the Urban Institute concluded that both the expansion and the new federal requirements led to funding constraints on "nutrition services and administration" that, in turn, led to scheduling less time per participant, increasing the use of group nutrition education (as opposed to individual sessions), and issuing standard food packages (as opposed to tailoring them to the individual needs of participants).

No wonder, then, that the limited evidence available suggests that participants still have major gaps in their knowledge of appropriate dietary practices. For example, a recent study of six WIC offices in three states, conducted by Mary Kay Fox and her colleagues at Abt Associates, found that although many participants had "reasonably high levels of nutrition knowledge," a substantial number still engaged in a number of inappropriate feeding practices.[16] More than 40 percent of the mothers "offered their babies something other than breast milk, formula, or plain water before the age of 4 months."[17] At some sites more than two-thirds reported doing so. Less than half of prenatal and postpartum participants said that they learned something from WIC.[18]

The fact that such practices continued, despite the parents' participation in WIC, should not be surprising. Counseling sessions are voluntary and, as Rossi concluded, "certainly inadequate for all but superficial instruction."[19] In fact, it appears that many parents choose not to participate. According to the Fox study, although most WIC participants were offered two nutrition education contacts each certification period, the number of contacts is actually much lower. For example, only 5 to 59 percent (depending on the site) of postpartum WIC participants received two contacts, because many participants failed to show up for scheduled nutrition education activities.[20] As the researchers concluded:

> These data demonstrate clearly that, while the amount of nutrition education offered is under the control of local WIC staff, the amount of nutrition education received is controlled by the individual WIC participant. It is fully dependent upon her willingness to participate in the nutrition education opportunities offered by the local agency.[21]

3

Program Coverage

Because of the relatively high income cutoff (almost twice the poverty line), loose interpretations of nutritional risk, and the fact that the middle class is having relatively fewer children than in the past compared with lower-income Americans, a surprisingly large proportion of Americans receive WIC benefits: nearly 50 percent of all infants, 25 percent of all children age one to four, and 25 percent of pregnant women. We estimate that another 10 percent of American children are eligible for benefits but do not receive them because WIC is not "fully funded"; that is, appropriations are not sufficient to provide services for all those who are statutorily eligible.[1]

Eligibility

Federal rules base eligibility for WIC on low income plus nutritional risk. Income eligibility is set at family incomes up to 185 percent of the poverty income guidelines ($31,543 for a family of four as of July 1, 2000).[2] Recipients of Temporary Assistance for Needy Families, food stamps, and Medicaid benefits are automatically deemed income-eligible.[3]

In addition to income eligibility, however, WIC recipients must be at nutritional risk. Eligibility for other major federal food programs usually is based solely on income. Nutritional risk is a broad concept that includes medical conditions like anemia, low weight, or overweight; a mother's age, history of pregnancy complications, or poor outcomes in prior pregnancies; and inadequate diet.[4]

WIC is not an entitlement program, another difference from other federal nutrition programs. Not all the people who fall within WIC's eligibility rules receive services because the program is not "fully funded" to that level of benefits. The number of women and children served in a given year is established by the amount Congress appropriates, with states free to add supplemental funding. Federal regulations require giving priority to pregnant and breastfeeding women and infants who have a nutritionally related medical condition, followed by other target groups and those with less severe nutritional risks.[5]

The application process for WIC benefits involves several steps that typically take about thirty minutes to complete. First, an applicant's income documentation is reviewed to determine financial eligibility. If the applicant is income-eligible, the next step is a nutrition certification, which is based on medical documentation and an abbreviated physical examination by a physician, nutritionist, nurse, or specially trained health care worker. The examination typically involves measuring the applicant's height and weight, reviewing the applicant's medical history, and drawing blood to test for anemia. The examination also includes an assessment of the applicant's dietary habits. If approved, participants must generally be recertified every six months, although pregnant women and infants may be certified for longer periods.

Until now, the process of determining nutritional risk appears to have been inexact at best. According to the Institute of Medicine's Committee on Scientific Evaluation of WIC Nutrition Risk Criteria, some states have used "generous" cutoff points and "loosely defined risk criteria." The committee concluded that "serious gaps in the evidence" existed for some of the risk criteria, with unreliable tools used to measure them.[6] Moreover, some of the criteria seem to have been loosely applied: "Street-level bureaucrats" were able to qualify someone who was marginally at risk or not at risk at all.[7] Although the extent of those problems is not known, effective April 1, 1999, the U.S. Department of Agriculture revised WIC's eligibility guidelines to tighten the process for determining nutritional risk.[8]

It is too early to tell whether the changes will affect front-line decisionmaking.[9] Our own analysis, described below, suggests that more often than not, agencies assume nutritional risk if the family meets WIC's income criteria. Moreover, it appears that even income determinations may not be as accurate as one would like. A 1988 USDA study of WIC participants estimated that 5.7 percent should not have been eligible because their income exceeded the maximum limit.[10] We speculate that the rapid growth in program participation since that time may have made the problem more pervasive today.

Program Participation

Always a popular program, WIC has grown rapidly. When Congress permanently authorized the program in 1974,[11] it served only 88,000 women and children at a cost of $10.4 million. Participation increased to nearly 2 million in 1980, at a cost of $725 million, and to 4.5 million in 1990, at a cost of $2.1 billion. In 1999 participation was near its all-time high, at 7.3 million, at a cost of $4 billion. If one also includes the rebates that infant formula manufacturers are pressured into giving, the program provides another $1.4 billion worth of food, for a total value of about $5.4 billion annually.[12]

In 1999 slightly more than half of all participants were children ages one through four, slightly more than a quarter were infants, and nearly a quarter were women, about half of whom were pregnant.[13] Spending by participant category was as follows: children, $2.05 billion; infants, $900 million ($2.33 billion if one includes the fair market value of the foods purchased with the rebate); and women, $1 billion.[14] Table 3-1 shows the historical growth in WIC expenditures and recipients.

Because eligibility is based on the vague concept of nutritional risk, it is difficult to gauge the actual size of the eligible population and, hence, the percentage of the eligible population that is participating. The best estimates come from the USDA Food and Nutrition Service; those estimates are based on health survey data and approximate the percentage of those with income eligibility who also have at least one nutritional risk. The USDA applies an estimate that "about 4 out of 5 income-eligible persons are also at nutritional risk and thus fully eligible for the WIC Program."[15]

On the basis of the USDA's estimates of the number of income-eligible families who are at nutritional risk, it appears that in 1997 about 87 percent of eligible people were participating. As table 3-2 shows, participation rates for pregnant women and older children were lower, 69 percent and 75 percent, respectively. But the figure for pregnant women is artificially depressed because it is estimated by using as the base all eligible pregnant women, from the very first week of pregnancy. Hence, even if all women participate for six months of their pregnancy, the participation rate would be just 65 percent. Most striking is the fact that 122 percent of the estimated number of eligible postpartum and breastfeeding mothers and 122 percent of the estimated number of eligible infants are participating.[16] We analyze that inconsistency in the next section.

Table 3-1   WIC Expenditures and Recipients, 1977–1999
(in millions of dollars and thousands of recipients)

Year	Expenditures (1999 dollars)	Women	Infants	Children	Total Recipients
1977	740	165	213	471	849
1978	984	240	308	633	1,181
1979	1,234	312	389	782	1,483
1980	1,499	411	507	995	1,913
1981	1,628	446	585	1,088	2,119
1982	1,644	478	623	1,088	2,189
1983	1,882	542	730	1,265	2,537
1984	2,231	657	825	1,563	3,045
1985	2,311	665	874	1,600	3,138
1986	2,394	712	945	1,655	3,312
1987	2,450	751	1,019	1,660	3,429
1988	2,549	815	1,095	1,683	3,593
1989	2,605	952	1,260	1,907	4,118
1990	2,734	1,035	1,413	2,069	4,517
1991	2,817	1,120	1,559	2,214	4,893
1992	3,050	1,222	1,684	2,505	5,411
1993	3,252	1,365	1,742	2,813	5,920
1994	3,551	1,499	1,786	3,192	6,477
1995	3,773	1,577	1,817	3,500	6,894
1996	3,922	1,648	1,827	3,712	7,188
1997	3,984	1,710	1,863	3,835	7,409
1998	3,971	1,733	1,883	3,749	7,365
1999	3,956	1,743	1,898	3,671	7,312

Note: Numbers may not sum owing to rounding.
Sources: *1998 Green Book* (U.S. House Committee on Ways and Means 1998); and *2000 Green Book* (U.S. House Committe on Ways and Means, 2000).

A significant drop-off in WIC participation occurs among families with older children. Theoretically, a mother who starts in a WIC program when she is pregnant should continue until her youngest child reaches age five if her income eligibility and nutritional risk continue. Participation drops off rapidly after the first year, however. For example, in 1998 nearly 2 million infants participated in the program, but only about 1.5 million one-year-old children did so. With each successive age group, participation fell, so that only 700,000 four-year-old children participated in the program.[17] See figure 3-1.

Although part of the drop-off may result from the difference in eligibility criteria for infants and children, as well as from the fact that family incomes tend to be higher as children grow older, we suspect that a

Table 3-2   WIC Participation as a Percentage of Eligible Persons, 1991–1997

Year	Pregnant Women (%)	Postpartum/ Breastfeeding (%)	Infants (%)	Children (%)	Total (%)
1991	61	47	91	44	56
1992	52	—	96	44	56
1993	52	79	98	48	60
1994	59	101	111	57	70
1995	58	105	109	64	75
1996	62	117	114	69	81
1997	69	122	122	75	87

Note: Because pregnant women are unlikely to participate in WIC for a full forty weeks, their participation rate is expected to be less than 100 percent. For example, if all eligible pregnant women enrolled in WIC for six months, their participation rate would be 65 percent.

According to the USDA, the high estimated participation rates for some groups (including over 100 percent for the postpartum/breastfeeding mothers and for infants) are due to differences between the way the number of income-eligibles is estimated and the certification practices applied in local WIC agencies. In addition, some imprecision is present in any survey-based estimate. The USDA concludes that "these data do strongly suggest that the program has likely achieved virtually full coverage of persons in this category at the national level."

Source: U.S. Department of Agriculture, Food and Nutrition Service, "Special Supplemental Nutrition Program for Women, Infants, and Children (WIC): Eligibility and Coverage Estimates," selected issues.

major contributor is the smaller value of the food package once the mother is no longer eligible to receive benefits for herself. For example, the value of a food package for a postpartum mother and her infant was worth about $120 per month, compared with just $34 for a child.[18] After a while, many mothers may simply decide that the small amount of food is not worth the time or trouble of continued participation. In a survey of WIC recipients, the supplemental foods that WIC provides were listed as the most attractive program attribute among mothers in the prenatal and postpartum components.[19]

Eligibility Creep?

Eligibility for WIC is set at 185 percent of the poverty line *plus* nutritional risk. As we saw, however, nutritional risk is an amorphous concept, and, as funding has increased, most agencies seem to have assumed that *all* income-eligible applicants are at nutritional risk.[20] Hence, in most places, eligibility essentially has become solely a matter of income.

Figure 3-1   WIC Enrollment of Children Age One to Four, Selected Years, 1984–1998

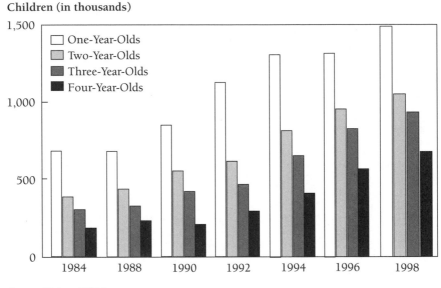

Source: Various USDA reports.

The priority system for vacancies is applied within that context. Moreover, as program funding has increased, according to some local WIC staff, even income testing seems to have become less rigorous, with many participants having incomes over eligibility limits. Remember, 122 percent of the estimated number of eligible postpartum and breastfeeding mothers and of eligible infants participated in WIC in 1997.

USDA estimates seem to confirm that "eligibility creep." For example, for various WIC target groups, the number of participants now exceeds the number who are income-eligible for the program. Between 1991 and 1997, the number of infants estimated to be eligible for WIC fell from 1.7 million to 1.5 million. During the same period, however, the number of infants in WIC rose from 1.6 million to 1.9 million, so that by the end of the period, according to the USDA's own data, 336,000 more infants were in WIC than were estimated to be eligible—22 percent over the estimate.

Many valid reasons exist for why more individuals participate in the program than are estimated to be eligible. For example, including Medicaid policies allows people with incomes above 185 percent of poverty to enroll in Medicaid and thus be eligible for WIC. In addition, prob-

Figure 3-2   WIC Coverage of Infants, 1982–1999

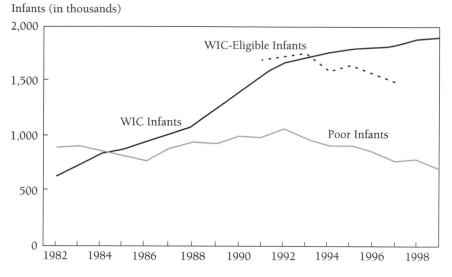

Infants (in thousands)

Source: Various USDA reports and the U.S. Bureau of the Census.

lems exist with the census data used to estimate income eligibility. Finally, differences exist between the family unit and income measures WIC agencies use and those the USDA uses to estimate eligibility.[21] But the larger point is that at the very least, all infants falling within the family income limits are now in the program. That means either that all infants under 185 percent of the poverty measure are at nutritional risk or that the criteria for nutritional risk are not being applied. Like many other observers, we believe that the latter explains the trend. At the same time, as mentioned above, some evidence indicates that determinations of income eligibility also are sometimes in error.

Similar trends apply to pregnant, breastfeeding, and postpartum women, and the same process is well on its way for children age one through four, with about 75 percent of the eligible population participating.[22]

Figures 3-2 and 3-3 portray the expansion in the number of WIC infants and children together with the number of poor infants/children in both groups. The figures suggest that the progression of expansion was from poor to less-poor infants and children, because the lines cross in 1984 and 1996, respectively; but the figures are also consistent with increased participation at all eligible income levels.

Data from the Survey of Income and Program Participation suggest that WIC's expansion has been primarily from low-income poor to those

Figure 3-3   WIC Coverage of Children, 1982–1999

Children (in thousands)

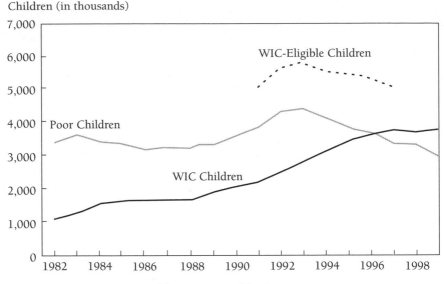

Source: Various USDA reports and the U.S. Bureau of the Census.

with relatively higher incomes. Richard Bavier of the U.S. Office of Management and Budget used the survey data to examine the distribution of WIC participants by income level in 1988 and 1996. He found that the percentage of WIC participants in families with annual incomes above $25,000 (measured in constant 1996 dollars) rose from 21 percent in 1988 to 29.4 percent in 1996, a 40 percent increase.[23] As Bavier noted, however, differences in the reporting of receipt of WIC benefits in the two years—with considerably higher reporting in 1996 than in 1988—compromised that analysis. It is unknown whether those differences bias the findings. Nevertheless, his findings are consistent with informal reports from the field and common sense. It appears that once the program reached those with the lowest incomes, agencies expanded eligibility by bringing in participants from higher-income families.

A number of explanations for the "eligibility creep" are possible. Outsiders do not understand the program and assume that because the statutory criteria require that recipients be at nutritional risk, all WIC families must need government aid. Insiders have been hesitant to raise the question, partly because they believe in the program and want its benefits to go to as many people as possible and partly because any suggestion that the program should be better targeted would suggest that the basic program requires improvement—and, of course, that would be inconsistent with the inflated benefit-cost estimates that have become part of the political landscape.

Feeding the process has been the unalloyed success of the infant formula rebate program, which has provided billions of dollars to WIC with little legislative oversight. In 1988 the rebates provided WIC with $32 million in additional funds that permitted the program to add 63,000 participants. In 1991 the rebates had grown to $650 million and fueled an increase in participation of nearly 1.1 million. By 1997 the rebates totaled $1.3 billion and added 1.9 million participants to WIC, roughly one-fourth of the program's entire caseload and one-third of its appropriated funding.[24]

Coming to the program outside the normal appropriations process, those billions of dollars have been automatically applied under WIC's eligibility and funding rules—without the administrators' considering whether the additional funds should be used to adjust program benefits or services. As a result, states have been forced to use those savings to expand participation, generally to those with higher incomes and lower nutritional risk, rather than to improve the program. Legitimate reasons exist for some limits in a program as large and diverse as WIC. But forcing states to add more and more families to the program is not one of them. In so doing, we have lost an opportunity to improve WIC's effectiveness by directing enhanced benefits and services to the neediest.

More expansions of WIC are looming. Everyone who is eligible for Medicaid is automatically deemed income-eligible for WIC. Recent legislation has allowed states to expand Medicaid to children in families with incomes above 185 percent of the poverty standard, which is also the WIC income limit. In response, twenty-two states have increased income-eligibility levels for Medicaid beyond 185 percent of poverty—generally to somewhere between 200 to 300 percent of poverty[25]—for at least one of WIC's target groups.[26] Hence, in many states, WIC eligibility is now greater than 185 percent of the poverty standard, which effectively increases the size and relative income of the WIC-eligible population. Other states are likely to follow suit.

4

Previous Research

A 1998 editorial about WIC in the *Washington Post* asserted that "repeated studies have shown that the program saves far more in health care costs than it spends."[1] The editorial went on to criticize congressional efforts to freeze enrollment and warned that "it makes no sense to apply that kind of constraint to this program. In the end, if the studies are to be believed, it will add to public costs."

We all would like WIC to be as successful as claimed. It also makes common sense that providing food packages and nutritional counseling to the poor ought to improve their diets. The plain and almost undisputed fact, however, is this: *Beyond modest reductions in anemia and modest increases in the intake of selected nutrients, little research evidence exists about the effectiveness of almost 90 percent of the funds expended under the WIC program.* The purported three-to-one savings calculation comes from research on the roughly 12 percent of the program that serves pregnant women. It is based on WIC as it existed more than a decade ago. Moreover, even that research is fraught with methodological uncertainty.

In the following pages, we review the research results for WIC, target group by target group. Much more research on WIC exists than we report here.[2] As Leighton Ku noted, "Many of the most interesting papers are not rigorous evaluations, but reports of field studies of descriptive analyses."[3] Hence, like Peter H. Rossi in *Feeding the Poor,* we have limited our discussion to studies that roughly meet accepted standards of scientific rigor. As we explain, however, even those studies are plagued by serious statistical concerns, largely around questions of selection bias, simultaneity bias, and generalizability.

Postpartum and Breastfeeding Mothers

About 12 percent of WIC participants are postpartum and breastfeeding mothers and account for about 13 percent of WIC spending. One would assume that nutritional supplements would aid such women or their next child, especially if the period between births is relatively short; but scant research exists on the impact of nutrition supplements on postpartum and breastfeeding mothers.

The only study that we could find on WIC's effects on postpartum mothers was conducted by Bette Caan of the School of Public Health, University of California at Berkeley, and her colleagues.[4] Using California administrative data from the 1980s, they evaluated the effect of WIC's postpartum benefits for women in California who gave birth to a child in the early 1980s and had a subsequent birth within three years. They found relatively small effects: For infants born to mothers who received WIC postpartum benefits for five to seven months between their two pregnancies, the mean birthweight was about 4 percent higher than for infants born to women who received postpartum benefits for less than three months or not at all. Women in both groups received WIC prenatal benefits during both pregnancies.

But questions of selection bias undermine the validity of even that small positive impact because the better-functioning mothers presumably sought the WIC benefits for a longer period. Another problem is that the researchers dropped about 20 percent of the original sample because of missing data, which could introduce attrition bias if, for example, the dropped cases had systematically different birth outcomes from those that remained.[5]

Some observers have suggested that the free infant formula that WIC provides may discourage breastfeeding, which is ordinarily considered better for newborns than consuming formula. Local WIC staffers often voice that concern. Although they encourage women to breastfeed, many believe that the free infant formula WIC provides—with a market value of about $80 a month—sends a powerful signal in the other direction, especially because an increasing number of WIC mothers have jobs, so it is more difficult for them to maintain a regular breastfeeding schedule. The research is not enlightening.

The National WIC Evaluation, conducted in the early 1980s by a group of researchers at the Albert Einstein College of Medicine in New York City and the Research Triangle Institute in North Carolina, compared the rate of breastfeeding of a nationally representative sample of

WIC participants at hospital discharge and that of a similarly low-income group of pregnant women not enrolled in WIC. After attempting to control for socioeconomic differences between the two groups, the evaluation found no statistically significant difference in the rates of breastfeeding between the two groups—58.8 percent versus 61.1 percent, respectively.[6]

A more recent study, also using nationally representative data and multivariate statistical techniques, compared the rates of breastfeeding initiation and the duration of breastfeeding between WIC participants and eligible nonparticipants.[7] Both prenatal WIC participants and eligible nonparticipants had comparable rates of breastfeeding—around 35 percent. Prenatal WIC participants who received advice about breastfeeding, however, had much higher rates than those who did not—44 percent versus 25 percent—although no difference in the duration of breastfeeding existed.

It is not clear how to interpret that finding. On the one hand, given the impact of counseling on the likelihood of breastfeeding, one might expect that counseling would also extend the average period of breastfeeding for mothers who would have done so without the counseling. On the other hand, the addition of some mothers who otherwise would not have breastfed may have reduced the period of breastfeeding if their commitment to breastfeeding were more tenuous.

In response to continuing concerns that WIC discourages breastfeeding, in 1993 the U.S. Department of Agriculture introduced an enhanced food package for breastfeeding mothers who forgo the infant formula food package. No rigorous research has been conducted on the reconfigured program. Thus, as Urban Institute researchers concluded in 1994, the most that can be said is that "it is not clear whether WIC promotes or hinders breastfeeding."[8]

Infants

About 25 percent of WIC participants are infants, who account for about 23 percent of spending, and again little research evidence of effectiveness exists. The National WIC Evaluation, conducted in the early 1980s and described above, is the most comprehensive examination of WIC's impact on infants and children.[9] The evaluation found that although infants participating in WIC did not have higher caloric intakes than those in the comparison group, they had higher mean intakes of certain nutrients, especially iron and vitamin C. WIC infants, however, had lower mean intakes of calcium, a factor that reflects that they were more likely to consume infant formula than whole milk. In addition, on a given day, significantly fewer WIC infants were likely to fall below 77 percent of the recommended dietary allowance for iron, vitamin A, and vitamin C.[10] They also were more likely to have a regular source of medical care and to be immunized than similar low-income children not on WIC.[11]

As Rossi concluded, however, the study was "plagued by a number of technical problems concerning the suitability of the comparison group used as well as severe response rate problems for both the WIC and comparison samples. Accordingly, the findings derived cannot be regarded as anything more than suggestive."[12]

Children

Half of all WIC participants are children ages one through four—the largest target group served by the program. That part of the program accounts for about 52 percent of expenditures. But here, too, the body of research on effectiveness is disappointingly sparse, with a few studies concluding that WIC reduced iron deficiency among poor children and modestly increased the intake of selected nutrients.

Again, the National WIC Evaluation found that children participating in WIC also did not have higher levels of caloric intake than the comparison group, but that they did have higher mean intakes of certain nutrients, especially iron and vitamin C. On a given day, fewer children were likely to fall below 77 percent of the recommended dietary allowance for iron and vitamin C.[13] The strongest positive dietary effects were for the least advantaged children, including those who were very poor and from female-headed households. No significant differences were found between past WIC participants and the comparison group, a result suggesting that WIC does not make long-term dietary improvements, whatever its short-term effects may be. WIC children also were more likely to be immunized and to have a regular source of medical care than similar low-income children not in the program.[14] As noted above for infants, however, we should view those findings as nothing more than suggestive because of technical problems related to the evaluation.

A 1998 study by Donald Rose of the USDA's Economic Research Service, Jean-Pierre Habicht of Cornell University, and Barbara L. Devaney of Mathematica Policy Research used the 1989–1991 Continuing Survey of Food Intake by Individuals to compare WIC preschoolers ages one through four in households with incomes below 130 percent of the poverty level with a similar group of preschoolers not in the program.[15] After attempting to control for differences in socioeconomic characteristics and possible selection bias, the study reported that WIC had statistically significant positive effects for ten of the fifteen nutrients examined, with particularly significant increases in the intake of iron and zinc (often lacking in the diets of WIC children).[16] Although the diets of most children already exceeded the recommended dietary allowances for many nutrients, those findings suggest significant dietary improvements for particular groups.

Unfortunately, that research suffers from the generic weaknesses of comparison group studies. Moreover, the considerable differences in the socioeconomic characteristics of WIC participants and the comparison group of eligible nonparticipants make it particularly difficult to judge how successfully the study controlled for those differences.[17]

Those studies, however, were conducted before the rapid expansion of WIC participation among children that occurred during the 1990s. A new study by USDA economists Victor Oliveira and Craig Gunderson, who used data from the 1994–1996 Continuing Survey of Food Intakes by Individuals, compared the nutrient intake of WIC preschoolers ages one through four in households with incomes below 200 percent of the poverty level with that of a similar group of preschoolers not in the program.[18] After attempting to control for observable differences in socioeconomic characteristics, the study reported that WIC had statistically significant positive effects for five of the eight nutrients examined—iron, vitamin C, vitamin A, vitamin B-6, and folate. But that analysis did not control for possible selection bias.

Recognizing that the two groups may have differed in unobservable ways, such as the nutritional motivation of the parents, the researchers attempted to control for possible selection bias by limiting their analysis to households in which a woman or infant was participating in WIC. From that group they compared the nutrient intake of WIC children and that of non-WIC children. Because all households had at least one WIC participant, the theory was that such a strategy would control for unobservable household characteristics including "nutritional awareness and motivation."[19] Using that sample, they reported that WIC has a significant positive effect on children's intake for three of the eight nutrients examined—iron, folate, and vitamin B-6. They suggested, however, that those findings understate WIC's impact, because the statistical model could not control for nutritional risk because of data limitations. It seems likely that the non-WIC children in the comparison group may have been less disadvantaged, particularly in terms of their nutritional risk.

There again, however, the generic weakness of comparison group studies and differences in the socioeconomic characteristics of WIC participants and the comparison group of eligible nonparticipants raise uncertainty about how well the study controlled for those differences.[20]

Ray Yip at the Centers for Disease Control and his colleagues took a different approach, using aggregate time-series data rather than comparison groups. With data from the centers' Pediatric Nutrition Surveillance System, they examined the incidence of anemia among children ages six months to sixty months who were enrolled in public health programs—primarily WIC.[21] The researchers limited their analysis to six states that consistently participated in the Pediatric Nutrition Surveillance System during the time period examined. Anemia among children ages six months to sixty months declined steadily from 7.8 percent in 1975 to 2.9 percent in 1985. Other studies report similar decreases.[22] The researchers examined trends separately for children seen at preenrollment screening visits and for those seen at follow-up visits.[23]

The decline in anemia for both groups could be a result of several factors. First, because the data are limited to children covered by programs such as WIC, the decline could have reflected a change in the composition of the group of children covered by the programs. For example, as WIC's funding and enrollment have expanded, the children in the program have probably become less disadvantaged. If the newly eligible children had lower rates of anemia than the earlier WIC recipients, they would have lowered the average rate of anemia, even if the WIC benefit itself had no effect.[24]

Second, the reduction may be part of a more general downward trend in iron-deficiency anemia caused by such factors as an increase in breastfeeding, the substitution of iron-fortified formula for unfortified formula and cow's milk, and general nutrition education efforts. WIC may also have contributed indirectly to the trend through its required iron fortification of many foods. As Devaney and her colleagues, who conducted some of the major WIC studies for Mathematica Policy Research, observed:

> WIC may also have had a role in reducing the prevalence of iron-deficiency anemia over time among all infants and children, including those who do not receive WIC. Because WIC vouchers constitute a large share of the market for infant formula and children's cereal, manufacturers may have changed the iron content of their products to meet WIC's eligibility requirements that include iron fortification.[25]

"Thus," Devaney added in another publication, "much of these foods that are on the shelves of supermarkets are iron-fortified and affect the diets of nonparticipants as well as program participants."[26] If that is the real explanation, a more direct way of achieving the beneficial effects on anemia claimed for WIC would be simply to require manufacturers to fortify infant formula, cereal, and bread.

But that is speculation. No study has successfully isolated WIC's impact from the changing socioeconomic characteristics of recipients or from the apparent secular decline in anemia.[27] Moreover, the existing studies are limited to a small number of states and therefore are not necessarily representative of the nation as a whole.

More important, the practical significance of those modest findings is unknown. If there had been a socially significant reduction in anemia, one would expect, for example, to see it reflected in a reduction in the behaviors associated with anemia. But as Devaney and her colleagues commented, "Little is known about the long-term effects of WIC on improving behavioral and cognitive development, outcomes that would presumably result from better iron nutrition status."[28] James Ohls, a senior researcher at Mathematica, echoed that thought:

> [C]ritics of the program correctly note that there is essentially no information available about the effects of the program on children in the one- to four-year-old range, the group currently "at the policy margin" in terms of how more (or less) funding would be used.[29]

Pregnant Women

The purported three-to-one savings calculation, cited by so many advocates and politicians, comes solely from research on one of the smallest parts of WIC, the program for pregnant women (12 percent of participants and 13 percent of expenditures). Giving impetus to that claim was a 1992 report from the General Accounting Office that reviewed seventeen "methodologically strong" evaluations of that part of WIC.[30] The GAO estimated that prenatal WIC participation resulted in a 25 percent reduction in low-birthweight births (under 2,500 grams) and a 44 percent reduction in very low birthweight births (under 1,500 grams).

Only one study examined the impact of WIC by using a random-assignment methodology. James Metcoff and his colleagues randomly assigned 471 women attending the prenatal clinics at the Oklahoma Memorial Hospital to WIC or to a control group.[31] WIC participation was associated with an increase in mean birthweight of 91 grams (2.9 percent). Despite the researchers' reliance on random assignment, WIC mothers were heavier than mothers in the control group at the time of entry into the study, so that they would be more likely to have heavier babies. When the researchers controlled for that difference, the birthweight finding was no longer statistically significant, except among mothers who smoked. (As we discuss below, that finding suggests the benefit of targeting WIC to women who are at greatest risk.) In any event, despite the study's rigorous methodology, the findings are not generalizable to the United States or the current WIC program, because the sample is drawn from a population receiving prenatal care in Oklahoma in the early 1980s.

One of the most influential studies the GAO reviewed was conducted by Devaney and her colleagues. In five states they matched 1987–1988 Medicaid and WIC records and then compared the outcomes of Medicaid recipients receiving WIC services with those not receiving WIC services.[32] After applying statistical controls for *identifiable* demographic and parental care characteristics that could also affect birth outcomes and Medicaid costs, the researchers found that WIC participants had fewer premature births and that their newborns had 1.6 percent to 3.8 percent higher birthweights (depending on the state).[33] Moreover, the researchers' estimates suggested a striking 28 percent decrease in the number of newborns with low birthweights and an even larger 59 percent decrease in the number of newborns with very low birthweights.[34]

Those apparent effects on birthweights have led to the belief that WIC saves money. Low birthweight and especially very low birthweight are linked to higher neonatal mortality and various childhood illnesses and disabilities.[35] According to one estimate, 35 percent of the amount spent on health care for infants consists of the added costs of providing medical care to low-birthweight infants, estimated to be about $15,000 more for each such birth in 1988.[36] If WIC reduces the incidence of low birthweight, it would reduce the need for subsequent Medicaid and other services and, thus, save money.

On the basis of the seventeen studies it reviewed, the GAO estimated that each dollar spent on WIC for pregnant women saved $3.50 (over an eighteen-year period) in Medicaid and disability payments paid by federal, state, and local governments and in medical care costs borne by private health care providers.[37] Here are the GAO's exact words:

[Every dollar] invested in WIC benefits returns an estimated $3.50 over 18 years in discounted present value, and $2.89 within the infants' first year to federal, state, and local governments and to private payers. Because GAO did not quantify all program benefits and estimate all potential cost savings at current eligibility and participation levels, savings may be greater than these estimates.[38]

Because the seventeen studies varied in quality and in the effects they found, the GAO's statement was actually a composite and weighted estimate of WIC's effects.[39] Moreover, the GAO did not measure the savings associated with WIC by examining reductions in Medicaid and other program costs directly, as some evaluations did.[40] Instead, the GAO estimated the savings in health care, disability, and special education costs associated with averting births with low and very low birthweights. It then applied that savings estimate to the estimate of the number of infants who were born at normal birthweight, rather than at low birthweight. That method erroneously assumed that averting a low-birthweight birth is the same as producing a birth with a normal birthweight. Many of the "averted" low-birthweight births may simply have moved from just below the 2,500 gram cutoff to just above it, a possibility suggesting that the actual savings would be much lower.

A deeper look at this body of research reveals more reasons why the GAO's conclusions should have been considerably more tentative. All but one of the studies the GAO reviewed were based on nonexperimental comparisons of WIC participants and nonparticipants, with statistical attempts made to control for other factors that influence birth outcomes. As we shall see, serious methodological problems with all the studies undercut their findings.

5

Research Weaknesses

As mentioned above, this review does not include all research on WIC. Excluded were those studies that failed to meet basic tests for validity or that provided insufficient information on which to make a judgment. But even those included in this review have weaknesses that require their findings to be considered highly uncertain. The three most significant weaknesses are selection bias, simultaneity bias, and lack of generalizability. Because the major WIC research tends to focus on the program's effects on pregnant women and their newborns, this chapter focuses on WIC's effectiveness as well.

Selection Bias

From a scientific standpoint, the preferred approach for measuring the effectiveness of WIC—or any social intervention—is a randomized experiment, where people eligible for WIC are randomly assigned to a treatment group (that receives WIC) and a control group (that does not). Properly implemented, random assignment should result in comparable treatment and control groups, so that any difference in subsequent outcomes can be attributed to the program rather than to some personal characteristic or external force that is systematically different in each group.[1]

Unfortunately for research, but fortunately for recipients, high percentages of eligible families now participate in WIC. On the mistaken belief that it would be necessary to deny benefits to currently eligible people—necessary for most randomized experiments[2]—most WIC studies have relied on statistical comparisons between those who received

WIC benefits and those who did not. Because participation in WIC is voluntary, however, some unobserved factor, such as parental motivation, may affect both participation and outcomes.

Here is the problem: If the pregnant women who voluntarily enroll in WIC are more concerned about their babies than those who do not, then their better birth outcomes may reflect their higher level of concern more than the program's nutritional counseling or food supplements. Conversely, if WIC recipients are at greater nutritional risk than nonparticipants, then comparisons with nonparticipants may understate the positive effects of WIC. Anne R. Gordon and Lyle Nelson of Mathematica Policy Research describe the two possibilities as follows:

> [S]ome pregnant women may not participate in the WIC Program because they lack access to or knowledge of publicly funded programs that provide health care or other services, which may independently affect birth outcomes. Thus, the estimated improvement in birth outcomes may overstate the effect of the Program since, relative to nonparticipants, WIC participants may have better outcomes even in the absence of the WIC Program. Conversely, if the WIC Program is successful at reaching high-risk, low-income pregnant women, WIC participants may be more likely than nonparticipants to have poor birth outcomes in the absence of the program. In this case, the estimated improvement in outcomes would understate the true effect of prenatal WIC participation. In either case, estimates are contaminated by selection bias.[3]

Careful regression analysis often can reduce selection bias, but even in the best circumstances it cannot do so completely. The results of a regression analysis are, however, of limited credibility when the differences between participants and nonparticipants are large and little data are available about their social, economic, and personality characteristics with which to explain differences in outcomes—as is the case in many WIC studies.[4] Joshua D. Angrist of the Massachusetts Institute of Technology and Alan B. Krueger of Princeton University have cautioned:

> A natural question about any regression control strategy is whether the estimates are highly sensitive to the inclusion of additional control variables. While one should always be wary of drawing causal inferences from a regression with observational data, sensitivity of regression results to changes in the set of control variables is an extra reason to wonder whether there might be unobserved covariates that would change the estimates even further.[5]

For example, no WIC study seems to have known the mother's marital status or age at first birth, possibly crucial determinants of her motivation and functioning.[6] Sometimes, even more basic information is unavailable. In their 1991 study of WIC's impact on low birthweight, for example, Barbara L. Devaney and her colleagues relied on data from birth records and several models to correct for selection bias. Although they did not describe the statistical models they used to correct for selection bias, they reported that the models "yielded very unrealistic results that were extremely sensitive to both minor changes in model specification and the estimation procedure employed."[7] As a result, they did not publish their selection-bias-adjusted findings.

The absence of realistic results should not be surprising. Devaney and her colleagues did not even have data on household income and, instead, had to rely on the mother's educational attainment as a proxy.[8] As a result, concluded Peter H. Rossi, "it may not have been possible to control for some differences in economic status between WIC recipients and nonrecipients."[9]

The problem of "omitted variables" is the reason many researchers say that they cannot determine whether selection bias understates—or exaggerates—WIC's effectiveness. In our experience, we find it much more plausible that the more motivated and higher-functioning mothers enroll themselves into the program, so that selection bias would tend to increase estimated effects. In 1986 Wayne F. Schramm wrote in *Public Health Reports*:

> As with other studies of this type, WIC mothers were self-selected in that they were motivated to apply for and receive WIC benefits. Other Medicaid mothers may not have been aware of WIC because Medicaid referrals were not as good in their counties. Still others probably had the same opportunity but were not motivated to apply for WIC. These mothers may have been less interested in health and nutrition, and these factors may have affected their infants' birth weights and Medicaid costs.[10]

If no other evidence existed, we would agree with those who say that it is impossible to gauge the amount of selection bias and that it could be quite small.[11] But recent studies persuade us that bias in the past studies is quite large and substantially exaggerates WIC's estimated impact.

Gordon and Nelson used data from the 1988 National Maternal and Infant Health Survey, a nationally representative source of information on the characteristics and experiences of women who had a live birth in 1988.[12] The researchers compared the birth outcomes of WIC recipients with those of income-eligible nonparticipants, but, again, the two groups differed on a number of demographic and socioeconomic characteristics, with WIC serving a generally more disadvantaged population.[13] Thus, statistical controls were needed to adjust for identifiable demographic, socioeconomic, and behavioral characteristics that also could affect birth outcomes.

After controlling for the *observable* characteristics of the two groups, Gordon and Nelson reported that WIC participants had infants with mean birthweights about 2 percent (68 grams) higher than infants in the comparison group. They also estimated that WIC reduced the incidence of low-birthweight newborns by 27 percent, from a mean of 10.8 percent without WIC to 7.9 percent with WIC. An even larger 45 percent reduction was estimated for very low birthweight births, from a mean of 2.2 percent without WIC to 1.2 percent with WIC.

To identify the impact of selection bias, Gordon tested their results by using three models to correct for selection bias: the Heckman two-step, or "Heckit," procedure; an instrumental variables estimator; and a maximum likelihood method.[14] Those tests are designed to measure the impact of nonrandom selection into the program through the use of "instrumental variables," that is, variables that explain program participation independent of factors that affect birth outcomes.[15] The instruments the researchers used to correct for selection bias were state WIC program food expenditures per capita,[16] a variable capturing whether the mother's family had any earned income,[17] and a variable indicating whether the mother had previously participated in WIC.[18]

If sample sizes are large enough and the models are well specified, that is, capable of explaining why people participate in the program, then each of those methods should produce similar estimates of WIC's impact.[19] The instruments are used, along with other observable characteristics of the mother, to predict WIC participation. The predicted participation is then substituted for actual participation in the statistical models to measure the impact of WIC on birth outcomes. As Rossi warned, however, "The success of this approach is heavily dependent on having good measures that relate to participation."[20] Unfortunately, that appears to have been a problem in Gordon's analysis, as her efforts resulted in widely divergent and inconsistent findings.

Unadjusted for selection bias, the estimated impact of WIC on mean birthweight was 70 grams. (See table 5-1.) But the three selection-bias tests (with slight variations in the instruments used) produced estimates ranging from a negative 307 grams to a positive 57 grams.[21] The Heckit procedure resulted in estimates that WIC reduced birthweight in amounts ranging from 371 to 89 grams. The instrumental variables approach led to estimates that WIC lowered birthweight in amounts ranging from 303 to 69 grams (although the latter estimate was not statistically significant). Finally, the maximum likelihood estimates were characterized as "unstable" and ranged from a reduction of 81 grams to an increase of 57 grams.

Gordon rejected those large negative estimates and instead adopted "as a premise that it is simply not possible that participation in WIC reduces newborn birthweight or related outcomes."[22] She did not believe that the estimates were reliable or that they should be used to draw any conclusions about the effects of WIC, even the direction of selection bias. Gordon may well be correct. It is, after all, her analysis, and in other places she and her colleagues provided a more extensive justification for rejecting the findings.[23] But given the parallels between her rejected findings and the findings of others—including, for example, those of Michael J. Brien and Christopher A. Swann discussed below—we find Gordon's results a strong sign that failure to control for selection bias overstates WIC's impact.[24]

Actually, it is theoretically possible that WIC reduces the mean birthweight of newborns. If WIC reduces infant mortality rates, the program may result in the survival of some low-birthweight babies who otherwise would not have lived. Although that reduces the mean birthweight of WIC infants, it is nevertheless a success for the program. That does not appear to have been the case in Gordon's study, however, since there was no statistically significant reduction in the infant mortality rate.

Those who have read a series of continuing analyses by Brien and Swann, who were formerly colleagues at the University of Virginia, believe that those analyses provide the best window into the uncertain effects of selection bias.[25] Like Gordon and Nelson, Brien and Swann used data from the live-birth sample of the National Maternal and Infant Health Survey. Unlike Gordon and Nelson, however, they added the infant death sample of the survey and further restricted their sample to non-Hispanic whites and non-Hispanic blacks. They selected WIC participants (the treatment group) and eligible nonparticipants (the comparison group) if they had family incomes below 250 percent of the poverty guidelines.

Brien and Swann estimated WIC's impact on birthweight by using a basic regression model with a variety of demographic, socioeconomic, and behavioral variables. Originally, they analyzed the impact of WIC for whites and blacks separately so that they could focus on "homogeneous"

Table 5-1 The Effect of Prenatal WIC Participation on Birthweight (grams/percent change)

Study	Regression Adjusted Impacts	Selection Bias Correction Impacts	Simultaneity Bias Correction Impacts	Selection + Simultaneity Bias Correction Impacts
Devaney, Bilheimer, and Schore (1990, 1991)	51[a] to 117[a]	"very unstable and unrealistic estimates"	11 to 60[b]	—

Gordon (1993) and Gordon and Nelson (1995)	70[a] (2.1%)	Estimation method:
		Heckit
		  Model 1 −371[a]
		  Model 2 −89[c]
		Instrumental variables
		  Model 1 −303[a]
		  Model 2 −69
		Maximum likelihood
		  Model 1 −81[a] to 47[a]
		  Model 2 57[a]
			Alternative definitions of WIC participation:
			  First 8 months 68[a]
			  First 7 months 53[b]
			  First 6 months 10
			Gestational cohorts:
			  28-week −4
			  32-week 28
			  36-week 27
			  40-week 39
			Controlling for gestational age: 25
				Estimation method:
				Heckit
				  Gest. age 28+ weeks −273[c]
				  Gest. age 32+ weeks −242[c]
				  Gest. age 36+ weeks −295[b]
				  Gest. age 40+ weeks −414[c]
				Instrumental variables
				  Gest. age 28+ weeks −314[c]
				  Gest. age 32+ weeks −242[c]
				  Gest. age 36+ weeks −314[b]
				  Gest. age 40+ weeks −307
				Maximum likelihood
				  Gest. age 28+ weeks −29
				  Gest. age 32+ weeks 23
				  Gest. age 36+ weeks 24
				  Gest. age 40+ week 9

Brien and Swann (1997)	Whites:
	  Model 1 54 (1.6%)
	  Model 2 91[a] (2.7%)
		Whites:
		2SLS
		  Model 1 178 (5.3%)
		  Model 2 228 (6.8%)
		Fixed effects
		  Model 1 (.3%)
				—

	Blacks:		Blacks:	
	Model 1	148[a] (4.8%)	2SLS	
	Model 2	117[a] (3.8%)	Model 1	421[a] (13.6%)
			Model 2	408[a] (13.2%)
			Fixed effects	
			Model 1	(4.9%[c])
Brien and Swann (1999b)	Whites:		Whites:	
	Model 1	34 (1.0%)	2SLS	
	Model 2	68[b] (2.0%)	Model 1	−153 (−4.5%)
	Model 3	82[b] (2.4%)	Model 2	−65 (−1.9%)
			Model 3	−248 (−7.3%)
			Model 4	−24 (−.7%)
			Fixed effects	
			Model 1	(−.3%[c])
	Blacks:		Blacks:	
	Model 1	173[a] (5.6%)	2SLS	
	Model 2	186[a] (6.0%)	Model 1	294[a] (9.5%)
	Model 3	146[a] (4.7%)	Model 2	195 (6.3%)
			Model 3	393[a] (12.7%)
			Model 4	266 (8.6%)
			Fixed effects	
			Model 1	(4.8%[a])

a. Coefficient is significantly different from zero at the 99 percent level in a two-tailed test.
b. Coefficient is significantly different from zero at the 95 percent level in a two-tailed test.
c. Coefficient is significantly different from zero at the 90 percent level in a two-tailed test.

groups. We asked them, however, to pool their sample of whites and blacks so that we could compare estimates of the program's impact for the population as a whole by using their approach to the estimates derived from the WIC evaluations described above. (The sample had too few Hispanics to permit a special analysis.) Brien and Swann's pooled analysis (unadjusted for selection bias and not presented in their paper) suggested that WIC increased birthweight by 2.3 percent.[26] Striking differences by subgroup existed. The results suggested that WIC increased birthweight by 4.7 to 6 percent for blacks and by 1 to 2.4 percent for whites, although the lower-bound estimate was not statistically significant.

Brien and Swann then attempted to correct for selection bias by using a variety of state-level instruments reflecting the generosity and availability of the WIC program in each state, which in turn may affect the chances of program participation.[27] They used the two-stage least squares technique to correct for selection bias, an approach equivalent to the instrumental variables method used by Gordon and Nelson. The result was to make WIC's estimated total impact no longer statistically significant. For blacks, however, estimated birthweight impacts increased between 9.5 and 12.7 percent in two of the models they used (although the findings were positive but not statistically significant in two other specifications). The estimates for whites, in contrast, became negative and statistically insignificant in all four specifications.

Brien and Swann hypothesized that their instruments might work better for blacks than for whites. That is possible, but in the context of research on the impact of programs similar to WIC and what we know about the national WIC program, we believe that it is more likely that the program is simply more effective for some subgroups than for others.

Thus, at least two sets of analyses, one by Brien and Swann and one by Gordon, made elaborate attempts to control for selection bias. In both cases, WIC's estimated positive birthweight effects disappeared for the population as a whole, a result suggesting that failure to control for selection bias overstates WIC's impact on birthweight and probably other related outcomes. Once again, it bears noting that Brien and Swann's findings also suggest that particular subgroups within the WIC population benefit from the program, perhaps substantially. (We describe their analyses in greater detail in the appendix.)

Simultaneity Bias

The longer a woman is pregnant, the more likely it is that her baby will be healthy. At the same time, though, the longer she is pregnant, the more likely it is that she will enroll in WIC—because she has more opportunities to learn about the program and more time to enroll. Thus, independent of any program effect, the positive birth outcomes for women who enroll in WIC late in their pregnancies are more likely attributable to the length of their pregnancy than to the effects of WIC—the program has little time to have any substantial impact, yet the baby is more likely to be born healthy. Failure to account for these "simultaneous" effects exaggerates WIC's estimated impact. Gordon and Nelson explained:

> [W]hile WIC participation may increase gestational age, causality may also operate in the opposite direction—in that a longer pregnancy may increase the likelihood of WIC participation. . . . Thus, the results of the basic model are likely to *overstate* the effects of WIC on birthweight and gestational age, and to overstate the reductions in low birthweight births, preterm births, and neonatal and infant mortality associated with WIC participation, because a portion of the estimated positive effects reflects reverse causality.[28]

But many WIC evaluations have ignored the problem of simultaneity bias and have therefore presented estimates likely to overstate the impact of the program. As Rossi commented, "WIC effects, although generally positive for birthweight and lowering the incidence of low and very low birthweight, are not likely to be as large as calculated in earlier studies since most of those studies did not control for the simultaneity problem."[29]

The few studies that have explored simultaneity bias show that it, too, substantially overstates WIC's estimated impacts. For example, Devaney and her colleagues attempted to control for gestational age by adding it as an independent variable to the birthweight and Medicaid cost regression equations.[30] Doing so provides estimates of WIC's effects on infants of a given gestational age and excludes any benefits associated with WIC's impact on increasing gestational age (to the extent that such impacts exist). As a result, estimated birthweight impacts were more than halved; they fell from gains of 51 to 117 grams to gains of 11 to 60 grams.[31] Estimated Medicaid savings declined to about 40 to 45 percent of the original estimates and resulted in a benefit-cost ratio of –$.87 to $2.29 (down from $1.77 to $3.13).[32]

Devaney and her colleagues also tried a second approach—redefining WIC participation by excluding very late WIC entrants. The researchers reclassified women who enrolled after thirty-six weeks and who redeemed less than $55 in food benefits as nonparticipants. That resulted in much smaller reductions from the unadjusted estimates—with estimated birthweight impacts ranging from 46 grams to 112 grams (a reduction of about 5 percent from the unadjusted estimates in most states) and a benefit-cost ratio of $1.38 to $3.[33] The change in estimated effects may have been small because that approach did not entirely eliminate the bias, because women whose pregnancies reach thirty-six weeks still have a longer period in which they can enroll in WIC (and thus be counted as WIC participants) than women whose pregnancies end earlier.

Gordon and Nelson applied more extensive corrections for simultaneity bias.[34] First, they controlled for gestational age by including it as an independent variable in their regression equations. The estimated impact of WIC on average birthweight for infants of a given gestational age was 25 grams, compared with the unadjusted estimate of 68 grams, although the result was not statistically significant. Second, they defined WIC participation in several ways, all of which were based on when a participant enrolled. For example, WIC participants were defined as those who enrolled in the program during the first six, seven, and eight months of participation.[35] Third, they created cohorts of women whose pregnancies reached a minimum number of weeks—twenty-eight, thirty-two, thirty-six, and forty.[36]

Thus, correcting for simultaneity bias reduced WIC's estimated impacts, but again, different approaches yielded different estimates. That uncertainty led Gordon and Nelson to present their resulting impact estimates of birth outcomes within ranges, rather than as precise estimates. For example, they estimated that WIC increased birthweight from 25 to 68 grams (approximately 1 to 2 percent of mean birthweight), reduced the incidence of low birthweight by 1 to 3 percentage points (from a mean of 10.8 percent), and lowered the percentage of preterm births by 2.4 to 3.6 percentage points (from a mean of 14.2 percent).[37] In fact, they found that WIC had no impacts on selected birth outcomes for some of their specifications (for example, for women who began participating in WIC during their first six months of pregnancy and whose pregnancies lasted at least twenty-eight weeks).[38]

More recently, Indu B. Ahluwalia and colleagues at the Centers for Disease Control controlled for simultaneity bias by looking only at full-term births.[39] They linked 1992 birth certificate data in Michigan to WIC participant files (achieving a match rate of 91 percent) to examine the impact of WIC on birthweight. Their findings suggest that WIC participation reduced small-for-gestational-age births and that the longer a woman participated in WIC, the greater the effect. For example, after controlling for the available sociodemographic and behavioral characteristics, they reported that mothers who began participating in WIC in the first twelve weeks of pregnancy were 28 percent less likely to have a low-birthweight baby. The findings are limited to one state (Michigan), however, and the authors cautioned that several important differences existed between WIC participants (who started participating in the first twelve weeks of pregnancy) and nonparticipants. For example, the WIC participants were more likely to be white (78 percent versus 60 percent) and to receive prenatal care in the first trimester (87 percent versus 66 percent) than nonparticipants. The authors noted, "Even though we controlled for several sociodemographic and behavioral characteristics, differences in other characteristics, such as the propensity to adopt healthful behaviors and seek services, could have biased our findings."[40] In other words, as in so many other studies, the authors did not address the possible role of selection bias.

We need two caveats to interpret those corrections for simultaneity bias. First, by effectively defining away any effect that WIC participation has on lengthening pregnancies, the corrections can understate WIC's impact. As Rossi cautioned, "It should be emphasized that controlling for gestational age may not be entirely appropriate because doing so may obscure WIC's positive effects on increasing gestational age."[41]

Second, the estimates are corrected only for simultaneity bias and, hence, still overestimate the effects of WIC, because they do not also correct for selection bias. When Gordon and Nelson attempted to control for both, they found large (statistically significant) negative effects when using the instrumental variables and Heckit approaches and very small (statistically insignificant) effects when using the maximum likelihood approach. As tables 5-1 and 5-2 show, however, studies rarely correct for both. If selection bias is exaggerating WIC's estimated impact, then the range of true impacts is even lower.

Lack of Generalizability

Another limitation of that research is that it may not be applicable to the national program, especially as it exists today. Many of the studies examine the WIC program in only one state or only a few states. Even if the findings are valid, it is an open question whether those states' experiences are representative of the nation as a whole. In fact, studies that look across states often find impacts that vary widely from state to state. Consider, for example, the five-state study conducted by Devaney and her colleagues. The estimated infant mortality rates associated with prenatal WIC participation were an almost incredible 45 percent lower in

Table 5-2 The Effect of Prenatal WIC Participation on the Incidence of Low Birthweight

Study	Regression Adjusted Impacts	Selection Bias Correction Impacts	Simultaneity Bias Correction Impacts	Selection + Simultaneity Bias Correction Impacts
Devaney, Bilheimer, and Schore (1990, 1991)	–22% to –32%[a]	—	—	—
Gordon (1993) and Gordon and Nelson (1995)	–27%[b]	Univariate probit model Model 1 79% Model 2 –5%	Gestational cohorts: 28-week –11% 32-week –13% 36-week –21%[a] 40-week –35%[a]	—
Brien and Swann (1997)	Whites: Model 1 .2 (3%) Model 2 –.1 (–2%) Blacks: Model 1 –5.4[b] (–39%) Model 2 –3.8[b] (–28%)	Whites: 2SLS Model 1 –3.5 (–54%) Model 2 –5.6 (–86%) Fixed effects Model 1 –.8 (–12%) Blacks: 2SLS Model 1 2.1 (15%) Model 2 3.9 (28%) Fixed effects Model 1 –4.2[b] (–30%)	—	—

Brien and Swann (1999b)

Whites:			Whites:		
Model 1	.2	(3%)	2SLS		
Model 2	-.2	(-3%)	Model 1	3.0	(47%)
Model 3	-.4	(-6%)	Model 2	1.0	(16%)
			Model 3	11.6[a]	(181%)
			Model 4	9.1	(142%)
			Fixed effects		
			Model 1	-.9	(-14%)
Blacks:			Blacks:		
Model 1	-5.4[b]	(-40%)	2SLS		
Model 2	-5.6[b]	(-41%)	Model 1	-7.9	(-58%)
Model 3	-3.9[b]	(-29%)	Model 2	-7.4	(-54%)
			Model 3	-7.5	(-55%)
			Model 4	-6.1	(-45%)
			Fixed effects		
			Model 1	-4.5[b]	(-33%)

a. Coefficient is significantly different from zero at the 95 percent level in a two-tailed test.
b. Coefficient is significantly different from zero at the 99 percent level in a two-tailed test.

three of five states studied.[42] There was no statistically significant impact in Minnesota, however, and in South Carolina the estimated reduction was so large (from 36.9 to 8.7 infant deaths per 1,000 live births, a reduction of 76 percent) that one of the authors of the study "expressed the opinion that the calculated effects . . . were likely overestimated."[43] Moreover, Gordon and Nelson, using a similar methodology but a national data set, could find no impact on infant mortality.[44]

In addition, all the studies are based on data collected more than a decade ago. (Some of the research on WIC's nonprenatal components is based on data that are almost two decades old.) Since then, important changes have occurred in the program and in the size, composition, and characteristics of the WIC population, all of which could affect the applicability of earlier research. Rossi pointed out:

> [W]hen programs expand, the characteristics of participants change, a shift that might affect effectiveness estimates. As WIC expands to cover a larger proportion of poor pregnant women, the women newly brought into the program may not have the same level of concern for the health of their fetuses or may not have as serious nutritional deficiencies.[45]

(As we note in chapter 3, it appears that as WIC has grown, application of the nutritional-risk criteria has become less rigorous.)

Moreover, many of the prenatal findings are restricted to mothers receiving Medicaid, which in 1988 represented only 46 percent of the caseload. Since those mothers were presumably from the most disadvantaged families in WIC, the findings may not be applicable to the non-Medicaid, and hence somewhat higher-income, families on WIC. Indeed, one study reported that WIC increased birthweight by an average of 106 grams for Medicaid recipients compared with only 62 grams for those not receiving Medicaid.[46] Thus, as Devaney and her colleagues explained in relation to their own study, the changes in Medicaid and WIC over time make it difficult to generalize from earlier studies to today's WIC program:

> Since the analysis period of the WIC/Medicaid study (1987), major changes have occurred in the Medicaid and WIC programs and in the environments in which these programs operate. Thus, the long-term stability of the study results is an important issue. Higher Medicaid income-eligibility ceilings for pregnant women, in conjunction with increased coordination between the Medicaid and WIC programs, means that a higher-income group of women is

likely to participate in the WIC programs. If prenatal WIC participation is more beneficial for lower-income women, then the benefits of prenatal WIC participation observed in 1987 may be greater
than what would be observed under the current Medicaid income-
eligibility standard for pregnant women of 133 percent of the federal poverty level. On the other hand, aggressive outreach,
streamlined eligibility procedures, and the growing problem of substance abuse may bring a higher-risk group of pregnant women
into both the Medicaid and WIC programs. The net effect of these
changes is uncertain.[47]

Finally, the world has changed. Mothers at the bottom of the income
scale are now more disorganized and subject to greater drug problems,
so helping them may be even more difficult than it was to help their
earlier counterparts, as Devaney and her colleagues observed as early as
in 1990:

> In particular, the increase in alcohol and drug abuse among preg-
> nant women—especially cocaine and crack—has become a major
> public health policy problem. While much of the information on
> this issue has been anecdotal, recent studies suggest that the num-
> ber of newborns exposed to drugs is increasing dramatically and
> that low-birthweight rates are thus rising.[48]

Accounting for Research Weaknesses

As we have seen, problems of selection bias, simultaneity bias, and
generalizability plague previous research. No objective way exists to
adjust for generalizability problems, but we can illustrate the impact of
selection and simultaneity bias. Tables 5-1 and 5-2 summarize the findings of the key birth-outcome studies. For the tables, we have not second-
guessed the researchers involved. If they asserted that they took steps to
deal with selection and simultaneity bias, we accepted their estimates
for the purpose of presentation. As the tables demonstrate, *both* selection and simultaneity bias are potent factors that we must consider in
assessing any research on WIC. It is on that basis that we reach the
judgments described next.

6

Does WIC "Work"?

Studies of WIC's impact are almost entirely nonexperimental; that is, they are based on statistical comparisons made between those who received WIC benefits and those who did not. As a result, many are subject to severe problems of selection and simultaneity bias. Nevertheless, many have been conducted by first-class researchers, and even their corrected findings on the program's impacts are usually positive, if often modest.[1] How, then, should we assess this body of research?

Modest Impacts at Best?

Careful researchers often present their findings about WIC's impacts as ranges. At the risk of great oversimplification, we have done the same for all the major studies described in this volume. (See table 6-1.) Doing so places WIC's possible impacts on infant mortality, prematurity, and birthweight on a range of from zero to substantial. For infants, children, and postpartum and breastfeeding mothers, the only impacts seem to be small to modest effects on anemia and nutrient intake. And, as we saw, the impacts on anemia could, at least in part, be explained by changes in the nutrient content of many foods.

In addition, a glimmer of evidence shows that WIC's beneficial effects are concentrated among the most needful recipients. David Rush and his colleagues reported that the strongest dietary effects were for the least advantaged children, including those who were very poor and from female-headed households.[2] Anne R. Gordon and Lyle Nelson also found that impacts on birthweight were greater for women receiving Medicaid than for those not receiving Medicaid. Women who received Medicaid

Table 6-1   Summarizing WIC Research

Newborns

Average birthweight: 0 to 4 percent
Low-birthweight rate: 0 to –30 percent
Very low birthweight rate: 0 to –55 percent
Preterm birth rate: 0 to –30 percent
Infant mortality rate: 0 to –66 percent
Neonatal mortality rate: 0 to –66 percent
Postneonatal mortality rate: 0 percent
Postpartum women (subsequent birthweight): 3 to 4 percent

Infants

Breastfeeding initiation and duration: insufficient evidence
Anemia: reduction, but not possible to quantify
Adequately immunized: 0 to 36 percent
Mean nutrient intake: vitamin C (59 percent) and iron (32 percent)

Children

Anemia: reduction, but not possible to quantify
Adequately immunized: 0 to 25 percent
Mean nutrient intake: positive for 1/3 to 2/3 of nutrients studied, most notably iron (about 20 percent) (two studies)

Note: Given the uncertainties of the research, past findings on WIC's impact are best expressed as ranges. Some studies have found and rejected negative or adverse impacts. For present purposes, so do we.

had lower average incomes than those who did not.[3] Finally, Michael J. Brien and Christopher A. Swann concluded that WIC had larger impacts on birthweight for blacks than for whites.[4] A comparison of their demographic characteristics suggests that the black women were poorer and more likely to be on welfare. Although those studies do not provide definitive proof that WIC is more effective for the most needful, they are suggestive.

Thus, in light of the research, about the most that one can say is that *WIC probably has "modest" impacts on some of its target populations*, depending on a host of demographic and community factors as well as the characteristics of the particular local program.

WIC probably makes at least a small improvement in the diets and behaviors of some pregnant women, especially the most disadvantaged; that, in turn, may improve the birth outcomes for some number of infants.

WIC probably increases the nutritional intake of some infants, especially those who would not have been breastfed, but the health consequences of the increases are not clear. Moreover, WIC may reduce breastfeeding, which can have negative health consequences.

In total, WIC probably makes little significant difference in the diets of one- to four-year-old children, but the average impacts may miss important effects for subgroups, especially for children whose intake of nutrients might otherwise be considered inadequate.

As this summary of key points suggests, existing WIC research, at least when read in the most favorable light, provides some—and perhaps substantial—support for the proposition that WIC has socially and policy-significant impacts on particular subgroups of participants. The research has not clearly established the makeup or identity of those subgroups, but the subgroups seem to comprise the most needful families—the poorest of the poor.

Those conclusions are based on data almost all of which is more than a decade old and on research involving a limited number of state programs. Thus, even that constrained conclusion is not necessarily applicable to the program as it exists today.

Others have similarly concluded that WIC's total impacts are likely modest, even in regard to what many see as WIC's most successful component, that for pregnant women. Brien and Swann, for example, concluded that "the existing literature finds mostly consistent evidence that the WIC program has a small positive effect on birth outcomes."[5] Robert L. Goldenberg and Dwight Rouse, writing in the *New England Journal of Medicine* in 1998, characterized WIC in the same way:

> The Special Supplementation [*sic*] Program for Women, Infants, and Children, which provides a calorically enriched diet to low-income pregnant women, has been in operation in the United States for more than 20 years. Studies of this and other caloric-supplementation programs in developed countries suggest that they result in small increases in birth weight.[6]

How much weight should we give to that judgment of "modest" results, since it is based on such ambiguous research? On the one hand, just because research cannot persuasively document that WIC has the large positive effects its partisans claim does not necessarily mean there are not any. Nutrition supplements and dietary counseling *should* make a difference in the lives of at least some disadvantaged mothers and children. Moreover, given the difficulty of conducting definitive research on programs like WIC, any research findings on WIC's impact would probably be somewhat equivocal (even with random assignment). Thus, we should take all findings—whether positive or negative—as suggestive at best.

On the other hand, it is difficult to believe that WIC's meager food and counseling benefits could have the large impacts claimed by advocates. The food packages, after all, average only about $46 per month in value (after including rebates), or about $1.50 a day, and they likely supplant, at least to some extent, food purchases the family would otherwise have made.[7] Moreover, some of the foods for older children undoubtedly end up being shared by the entire family, a practice that minimizes the effectiveness of the program for the group being targeted. Gustavo J. Arcia and his colleagues at the Research Triangle Institute and the National Opinion Research Center, for example, found that participation in WIC did not increase total food expenditures, a finding that supports the view that WIC functions at least somewhat as an income transfer program, although it did appear to shift such expenditures to more nutritious foods.[8] Last, a recent General Accounting Office report indicated that a small number of WIC participants exchanged their vouchers for nonapproved or nonfood items, traded them for cash, or gave them away.[9] In addition, the nutritional counseling only amounts to fifteen to thirty minutes every six months.

Moreover, such large effects would be inconsistent with research in related areas. For example, a body of research on the impact of nutrition supplements on birth outcomes suggests the conclusion that *only severely undernourished pregnant women obtain substantial benefit from nutritional supplements.*[10] University of Oxford epidemiologist Fiona Mathews and her colleagues studied the dietary patterns of 693 first-time mothers during pregnancy and concluded that "among reasonably well-nourished women of industrialized countries, however, maternal diet in pregnancy has, at most, a small impact on placental and birth weights."[11]

Thus, in an introduction to a volume on research concerning low birthweight, Patricia H. Shiono and Richard E. Behrman, at the time both at the Packard Center for the Future of Children, concluded, "Because very few women in the United States are severely undernourished, only a small subset of women might be helped by dietary interventions."[12] If that research validly applies to the population of WIC recipients, and if the large impacts claimed for WIC are to be believed, then some substantial portion of the pregnant women receiving WIC benefits must have been "severely undernourished." But no evidence exists that they were undernourished.

Nor has parallel research documented the ability of nutrition education to improve birth outcomes. For example, after reviewing the "equivocal research findings regarding the impact of supplementation on birthweight in adequately nourished populations," Greg R. Alexander of the University of Minnesota and Carol S. Korenbrot of the University of California at San Francisco asserted that it is unlikely that "assessment and counseling efforts alone will be highly associated with birth weight improvements."[13]

So, too, is the case for prenatal care programs, which can encompass medical, educational, nutritional, and other social services. Although a general belief exists that prenatal care is beneficial to both mother and child, the empirical evidence regarding the impact of prenatal care is mixed. In a review of the literature, Alexander and Korenbrot concluded:

> The collective evidence suggests that adequate prenatal care is associated with reduced rates of low birth weight but mainly among more mature full-term infants. Unfortunately, prenatal care has not been shown to prevent fetal growth retardation among less mature preterm infants or to prevent preterm birth. The relationship between prenatal care and very low birth weight (less than 1,500 grams, or 3 pounds, 5 ounces) and very preterm delivery (at less than 33 weeks) is also uncertain.[14]

Finally, there is the apparent lack of success of the federal government's Healthy Start Program, begun in 1991 to test innovative ways to reduce infant mortality in fifteen areas of the country where infant mortality is a serious problem. Healthy Start provides many of the same services that WIC does, such as nutrition education and referral to other agencies. Although Healthy Start does not provide a food package, it does direct participants to the WIC program. After the third year of program operations, an interim evaluation reported that Healthy Start had little or no effect on infant mortality, low birthweight, very low birthweight, and preterm birth rates.[15]

Taking everything into consideration, then, we judge that WIC probably does make "modest" improvements in the health and well-being of at least some groups of disadvantaged children and their mothers. And, as described above, its effectiveness probably depends on a host of demographic and community factors—and the characteristics of the particular local program.

What does our reassessment suggest about WIC's benefits in relation to its costs? First, we have found no responsible authority that claims that the 90 percent of the WIC program for infants, children, and postpartum and breastfeeding mothers produces savings that exceed the associated costs. And, if WIC's impacts on pregnant women and their newborns are only "modest," then it is unlikely that even that component of the program could pass any real benefit-cost test.

Furthermore, when Barbara L. Devaney and her colleagues took just simultaneity bias (and not selection bias) into account, estimated Medicaid savings fell 60 percent from the original estimates and resulted in a benefit-cost ratio of –$.87 to $2.29 (down from $1.77 to $3.13).[16] Likewise, Brien and Swann found that controlling for selection bias (but not simultaneity bias) resulted in smaller benefit-cost effects than those estimated by the GAO.[17] They concluded that "the program is not cost-effective for whites."[18] For blacks, however, their findings suggested a savings of $1.57 to $3.50 per dollar spent on WIC, but even those findings were based on estimated reductions in the incidence of low birthweight that were not statistically significant.

Taken together, then, those studies strongly suggest that WIC's overall benefit-cost ratio, even for the prenatal component, is considerably less than the three-to-one ratio estimated by the GAO and cited by advocates—and is quite possibly negative.

The Need for a New General Accounting Office Estimate

In 1992, as described above, a GAO report estimated that prenatal participation in WIC reduced low-birthweight births by 25 percent and very low birthweight births by 44 percent—so that each dollar spent on WIC for pregnant women saved $3.50 (over an eighteen-year period) in medical and disability costs. That GAO report legitimized the claims of advocates that WIC "worked." After all, if the GAO said so, then WIC really must be a success.

WIC partisans use those GAO estimates on pregnant women and their newborns as if they were undebatable—and as if they applied to the entire WIC program. Here is a 1998 quotation from the *prepared* remarks of Shirley R. Watkins, undersecretary for Food and Nutrition and Consumer Services, who should have known better:

> We can still say that for every $1 in WIC, $3 is saved in Medicare [*sic*] costs. These are numbers that people can relate to and understand in very real terms, and we should use every opportunity to tell people about how successful this program is, not just for mothers and babies, but for everyone.[19]

Sometimes the GAO finding is explicitly but misleadingly used to give an overblown impression of WIC's impact, as illustrated by this 1997 statement from the Center on Budget and Policy Priorities:

The WIC program is probably the single most successful of all federal social programs. Extensive medical research has found that WIC reduces low birthweight, infant mortality and anemia and improves diets. . . . The GAO reported that each dollar expended in the prenatal component of WIC averted $3.50 in expenditures for Medicaid, SSI [Supplemental Security Income] for disabled children, and other programs.[20]

Those claims get repeated, in turn, by politicians who are too busy to look beyond the fact that there indeed was a GAO report.

A more subtle effect of the GAO's seal of approval has been to freeze the program in time. After all, goes the thinking, if the program works, why spend money studying its impact—and why engage in the politically difficult task of programmatic improvement?

The GAO should conduct a new benefit-cost assessment of WIC. In 1992, when the Bush administration's U.S. Department of Agriculture reviewed a prepublication version of the GAO report, it raised concerns about the GAO's methodology and suggested that its estimates may have exaggerated WIC's impact. Here is the GAO's summary of the USDA's comments, many of which echo points made in this volume:

USDA expressed concern that we overestimated cost savings attributable to WIC because certain of our model's assumptions might not hold. They were concerned that our model did not capture all of the program's positive and negative effects and depended upon evaluations that themselves may not have accurately separated program effects from all measured and unmeasured differences between WIC and non-WIC populations. They also said that the calculated reduction in low-birthweight rates due to WIC based on the evaluations we used might not represent the true national effect of WIC, and that the evaluations used to develop the effect size were dated in that characteristics of the WIC population had changed.[21]

Unfortunately, those concerns seem to have been discounted as being ideologically based and were lost in the din of support for WIC.

Whatever the wisdom of the GAO's initial judgment about WIC's benefit-cost ratio, our review of the research strongly suggests that it is time for the GAO to reconsider its estimates and, in particular, to make the appropriate adjustments for selection bias, simultaneity bias, and lack of generalizability—or that it conclude, as it did in regard to Head Start research, that no reliable estimate can be made.[22]

Taking that step would be consistent with the GAO's evaluation criteria for other programmatic research. For example, the GAO's 1997 assessment of Head Start research rejected the findings of many studies because of methodological problems, particularly selection bias and lack of generalizability:

> One of the most serious of the methodological problems was noncomparability of comparison groups. The most reliable way to determine program impact is to compare a group of Head Start participants with an equivalent group of nonparticipants. The preferred method for establishing that the groups are equivalent at the outset is to randomly assign participants to either the Head Start group or the comparison group. . . . In most cases, researchers matched participants on one or more demographic variables, usually by including some variable related to socioeconomic level. In other cases, researchers did not match treatment and comparison groups but tried to compensate statistically for any inequality between the groups. Neither of these methods compensates for lack of random assignment to group.[23]

The GAO's conclusion was that, as a result of those and other weaknesses, the research provided little information on the program's impact. Applying the same rigorous standards to the WIC research might lead to a different conclusion from the one that the agency reached in 1992.

In addition, the GAO should consider altering the manner in which it calculates the savings estimate. The GAO used an unsupported assumption that all the added costs of low-birthweight births can be avoided for each such birth averted. If WIC's real effect is to raise birthweights from just below the 2,500 gram cutoff point for being classified as "low" birthweight to just above it, the savings were probably exaggerated, because such births would generally result in higher costs than normal birthweight births.

Researchers at the RAND Corporation described how sensitive savings are to changes in birthweight:

> [I]nterventions that simply shift very low birthweight infants into higher weight categories can save substantial amounts. An increase of 250 grams saves an average of $12,000–$16,000 in the first year. An increase of 500 grams generates savings of $28,000.
>
> However, not all increases in birthweight produce cost savings. At the lowest birthweights, added weight can increase treatment costs because the infant is likely to live longer and require a lengthier

hospitalization. Thus, an increase in birthweight from less than 750 grams to between 750 and 999 grams would actually increase treatment cost by $29,300; an increase to the 1,000–1,249 gram range would increase costs by $13,500.[24]

If possible, the GAO should use more fine-grained estimation methods that recognize those complexities. It might also state its estimates as a range, as do many other researchers in this field.

Finally, the GAO should recognize the diversity of WIC's caseload and examine the possible variation in benefit-cost ratios for different subgroups. A recent report by Lynn Karoly and her colleagues at RAND estimated the economic impact of a nurse home-visitors program (described in more detail in chapter 7). Their findings suggest that the program produced large net savings from serving higher-risk families (single mothers of low socioeconomic status), but that no net savings associated with serving lower-risk families (mothers who were married and of higher socioeconomic status) existed. Here is what they said:

> For the . . . higher-risk families of the Elmira [program], our best estimates of the savings to government are much higher than the costs. . . . In the case of the lower-risk participants of the Elmira [program], the savings to government are unlikely to exceed the costs. In fact, our best estimate of the net savings is that they are negative: The government savings, while positive, are not enough to offset program costs. This result illustrates the importance of targeting programs to those who will benefit most if the hope is to realize government savings that exceed costs.[25]

The Need to Address Overweight

Deciding whether WIC works requires identifying the problem it should be addressing. When WIC was being planned almost thirty years ago, "hunger and malnutrition constitute[d] a national emergency," in the words of the 1969 White House Conference on Food, Nutrition, and Health.[26] Experts disagree about the extent of hunger—the issue has long been politically contentious—but few doubt that it was a serious problem in the past and that it is much less serious now.

Conversely, for the past three decades, the prevalence of overweight and obesity among Americans has steadily increased. Most determinations of overweight are based on the body mass index, which describes body weight relative to height. For adults, a body mass index between 25.0 and 25.9 is considered "overweight," and an index of 30.0 or greater is considered "obese." In 1999 61 percent of adults were classified as overweight or obese. Former Surgeon General C. Everett Koop observed that "[t]his high incidence of obesity is particularly pronounced in minority populations, especially among women, and is rampant among low-income ethnic populations."[27] Moreover, the problem has been worsening, as the incidence of overweight and obesity is up about one-third from the late 1970s, with most of the increase coming from the near doubling of obesity, which grew from 15 to 27 percent.[28]

The criteria for overweight for children are somewhat different from those for adults. In general, children with body mass indexes above the ninety-fifth percentile on charts measuring body mass index by age and growth are categorized as overweight. On the basis of that measure, the prevalence of overweight among children of ages six through nineteen has increased from 4 to 5 percent in the 1960s to 13 to 14 percent in 1999, with the most dramatic increase occurring after 1980.[29] Other researchers have used the eighty-fifth percentile, which results in estimates of overweight exceeding 20 percent.[30] Similar increases in the prevalence of overweight have been reported for preschoolers, with the percentage overweight or obese increasing from 18.6 percent in 1983 to 21.6 percent in 1995, with a corresponding increase in obesity from 8.5 to 10.2 percent during the same time period. Since overweight children are more likely to be overweight as adults, those increases are a public health concern of the first order. About 22 percent of children ages six to seventeen were overweight compared with just 1 percent of children under eighteen who reported hunger.[31]

In general, overweight appears to be most serious among the poor and those in lower socioeconomic groups.[32] For example, 33 percent of adults reported being overweight, while only 4 percent of households reported having one or more adults who repeatedly experienced reduced food intake that resulted in "the physical sensation of hunger."[33] Only 13 percent of poor households reported "hunger," even with that very broad definition.[34] A recent study reported that the highest overweight and obesity rates were among low-income adolescents—Mexican American males ages six through eleven and African American females ages six through nineteen, but the increases have affected children of all ages and races.[35]

Former Agriculture Secretary Dan Glickman commented on the implications of the striking change from "too little" to "too much" food:

The simple fact is that more people die in the United States of too much food than of too little, and the habits that lead to this epidemic become ingrained at an early age.

Everyone here knows the statistics: Obesity and overweight affect 10 million U.S. children. That's a record, and there's no real sign that it won't be broken again soon. In the past 20 years, the number of obese children has doubled, placing more Americans at risk of high cholesterol, blood pressure, heart disease, diabetes, arthritis and cancer—all at an earlier age.

Obesity contributes to 300,000 deaths each year. That's close to 1,000 lives lost each day at a cost to our health care system of $70 billion a year, or 8% of all medical bills.[36]

Those trends are reflected among WIC recipients. Devaney of Mathematica Policy Research, using data from the third National Health and Nutrition Examination Survey, a national study of the health and nutrition status of the civilian population conducted between 1988 and 1994, found that a substantially larger proportion of WIC children and women are overweight compared with the general population.[37] They are also less likely to be underweight.

Obesity is linked to many adverse health outcomes, including increased mortality, coronary heart disease, hypertension, diabetes, gallbladder disease, osteoarthritis, and some cancers.[38] In children, it can lead to serious health problems in later life. According to physicians at the Children's Hospital at Dartmouth College, who conducted an extensive review of the long-term health consequences of early behaviors:

Childhood and adolescent obesity is increasing in prevalence, and obesity has profound medical and psychosocial consequences for children and adolescents. Obese children are at greater risk for hypertension, respiratory disease, diabetes, and various types of orthopedic problems, particularly slipped capital femoral epiphyses. Individuals who are obese as adolescents experience approximately twice the rate of mortality on long-term follow-up compared with those who are not obese. Morbidity from causes as diverse as coronary artery disease, colorectal cancer, gout, and arthritis is increased in cohorts that are obese as adolescents. Obesity in childhood increases the risk of subsequent morbidity regardless of whether obesity persists into adulthood. Psychosocial morbidities of adolescent obesity can be profound. In a recent U.S. study, young people 16–24 years of age who were obese completed fewer years of school, were less likely to get married, had lower household incomes, and were more likely to be living in poverty than those who were not obese when followed-up after 7 years.[39]

Writing in *Pediatrics,* James Hill of the Department of Pediatrics at the University of Colorado Health Sciences Center and Frederick Trowbridge of the Nutrition and Health Program at the International Life Sciences Institute in Atlanta warned that the health problems associated with obesity will become more obvious as the population ages and therefore stressed the need to address the issue now:

> The threat of obesity is greater than ever for U.S. children and adolescents. All indications are that the current generation of children will grow into the most obese generation of adults in history. Furthermore, there is every expectation that the next generation of children is likely to be fatter and less fit than the current generation. Despite the recognition of the severe health and psychosocial damage done by childhood obesity, it remains low on the public agenda of important issues facing policy makers. Perhaps this is because the most serious health effects of obesity in today's children will not be seen for several decades. Action must be taken now to stem the epidemic of childhood obesity. This action will require a prioritization of research into the etiology, treatment, and prevention of childhood obesity. It is unlikely that sufficient resources for such research will be available from public and private sources until the issue of childhood obesity is moved higher on the public agenda.[40]

Efforts to combat overweight should become an express element of WIC's mission. The WIC program is not oblivious to the dangers of obesity and overweight to low-income Americans. Indeed, overweight is one of the nutritional risk criteria used in determining eligibility for benefits. The plain fact, however, is that the program's basic orientation is toward increasing food consumption, albeit healthier consumption. For example, current WIC regulations largely ignore the problem, except in relation to the nutritional risk criteria—but not to services or objectives.

If combating overweight were an *expressed* element of WIC's mission, the USDA would be encouraged to manage toward that objective—and evaluations of the program would be more likely to assess WIC's impact on obesity. Therefore, we conclude that efforts to combat overweight should become an express element of WIC's mission.

7

Programmatic Flexibility

How should responsible policymakers respond to the fact that WIC's impacts are probably modest at best? Certainly not by simple-mindedly cutting or abandoning the program. The problems that WIC addresses are serious and require attention. In an age when so many government programs for the poor seem to have no effect and may even make things worse,[1] WIC's possible beneficial effects should not be slighted. But, just as certainly, policymakers should not continue the program without trying to improve it. Nutrition-related health problems are still serious and widespread, although they now also involve high levels of overweight. If WIC can be made more effective, we should strive to make it so.

Unfortunately, no one really knows how to make WIC more effective. Partly because it has been so politically incorrect to acknowledge the limitations of previous research, researchers and policymakers have not conducted necessary studies and planning. A good way to begin would be to open the program to innovation and experimentation.

WIC was established in 1972, and since then its essential shape has been frozen in place. State and local officials are relatively straightjacketed by various federal rules—even though those individuals are presumably in the best position to judge whether various program adjustments are needed. Simply put, local health departments, hospitals, public health clinics, and community health centers should have more freedom to try new approaches.

The mechanism for giving those institutions greater programmatic flexibility could be direct statutory grants of discretion or a legislatively authorized, case-by-case waiver process. For example, the National Association of WIC Directors has called for such "regulatory waivers for the purpose of testing alternative service delivery projects and food prescriptions."[2]

Here are just a few of the program variations that should be allowed. Any changes should be fully and rigorously evaluated, as we describe in chapter 8. No certainty exists that the ideas will work, so each is expressed as a question to emphasize its tentativeness.

Target WIC Benefits to More Needful Families?

As described above, WIC participants include nearly 50 percent of all infants, 25 percent of all children ages one to four, and 25 percent of pregnant women. Because household incomes vary from state to state, in six states as many as 60 percent or more of all newborns receive benefits.[3] About 50 percent of all infant formula sold in the United States is purchased with WIC dollars.[4]

Implicit in current coverage of the entire WIC program is the judgment that nearly 40 percent of all American children are at nutritional risk— and that their mothers need corrective counseling. That cannot be right.

Essentially, WIC funding has increased far in excess of what can be effectively used under current eligibility rules. Spending rules are also part of the problem, as we next describe. Our analysis in chapter 3 suggests that recent WIC expansions have primarily been among those with higher incomes and relatively less nutritional risk. As researchers at the Urban Institute pointed out in 1994, "As the Program expands, much of the new caseload will come from increases in participation by children and postpartum women, the two categories with lowest priority now."[5]

We believe that the eligibility creep has been excessive and that there should be a cutback at the upper levels of income eligibility. Actually, policymakers should conduct a top-to-bottom reevaluation of WIC's eligibility criteria. According to a committee of the Institute of Medicine, current funding priorities may force states to deny access to some individuals to serve others who are in less need of the program's benefits:

> Many individuals now classified in low priority categories have more potential to benefit from WIC services than some individuals placed in higher priority categories. For example, a child of a mentally retarded parent (currently priority VII) or an anemic child age 3 years with a very low hemoglobin level (currently priority III) may have a greater potential to benefit than an infant classified as anemic (currently priority I) by a criterion with a too generous cutoff point.[6]

The funding that now goes to lower-risk recipients could be redirected to make improvements in the basic program *for more needful families*—primarily by either intensifying services or expanding their duration. We discuss both options below.

Selectively Intensify WIC Benefits?

As the research discussed in this volume suggests, WIC's positive effects are probably concentrated among its most disadvantaged recipients. As chapter 2 shows, the result of federal rules is essentially to require that all recipients in the same target group receive basically the same set of WIC benefits, notwithstanding their differences in need. States and local agencies administering the program cannot make real changes in benefits to meet the palpably different needs of clients. Remember, WIC agencies are prohibited from expanding the amount of the food packages given.

Why does the program have such limitations? They were perhaps understandable when the program was much smaller—and funding was limited. But surely a family on welfare might need more food than a family at the top of income eligibility, which can exceed $50,000 for a family of eight. About a third of WIC families have annual incomes over $25,000; they have very different (and lesser) needs than those with incomes below $10,000. Why not allow states, at least on an experimental basis, to increase the size of the food package for the most needful families?

And, just as surely, $12 per month for nutritional counseling and education (as well as for administrative costs) is insufficient to meet the needs of some families. For example, enhanced nutrition education services could be directed to families with obese children or children who have a predisposition to cardiovascular disease or high cholesterol. Likewise, additional services could be provided to parents with a drug- or alcohol-abuse problem. In California, a number of local WIC agencies have begun targeting special populations, such as teens and smokers, presumably because of their greater risks of adverse birth outcomes.[7] They have, however, had to use other sources of funding to provide such program enhancements.

Making WIC counseling sessions more relevant would involve major—and expensive—programmatic changes. A comprehensive review of nutrition education programs for pregnant women and mothers with infants, led by Isobel Contento of Columbia University and published in a special issue of the *Journal of Nutrition Education*, concluded that "such interventions are effective when they focus on the pregnant woman's specific needs and provide follow-up sessions to reinforce and maintain behavioral changes."[8] For example, the study reported gains in maternal and infant weight from nutrition education classes that "were augmented with multiple individual counseling sessions."[9]

Janet Schiller, the U.S. Department of Agriculture project officer for many WIC studies, and Mary Kay Fox, a long-time WIC researcher at Abt Associates, described suggestions from the WIC community for improving the program: using incentives to change behavior; giving clients greater choice in the selection of classes; improving communication with health care providers; enhancing training opportunities for nutrition educators; and including fathers and grandmothers.[10] In our own visits to WIC centers, we have been told of the need for more cooking demonstrations, with special attention given to the needs of recent immigrants. Along similar lines, Shannon E. Whaley of the University of California at Los Angeles and Laurie True of the California WIC Association argued for expanding WIC's nutrition topics to include those that are relevant to parenting and child development.[11]

Local agencies are legally authorized to implement many of those ideas, but WIC's current spending restrictions, along with federal mandates on the content of services (such as voter registration), constrain their ability to do so. Although states can theoretically vary the amount they spend on counseling per participant, total spending for "nutrition services and administrative" costs is capped. Because all WIC recipients must get a minimum level of services under the $12 cap, not enough funding is available to intensify services in any meaningful way.

Allow States to Spend More on WIC Benefits and Services. Instead of adding more people to the rolls, it might make sense to change WIC's rules to allow local agencies to provide more food benefits and educational services to poorer families who palpably need more aid than those at higher incomes. Once again, those expansions need not—in fact, should not—be across-the-board. States do not need a larger but one-size-fits-all program.

Add a Focus on Preventing Overweight?

Most experts believe that the best approach to combating overweight is preventive, because treatment is so problematic, as described by researchers at the Centers for Disease Control:

Treatment of obesity for adults has been shown to be largely ineffective. Dietary treatment of children and adolescents is further complicated by possible interference with growth. Therefore, it is crucial to focus on prevention of overweight among youths. Attempts to increase physical activity for children and adolescents may provide a promising avenue in this effort.[12]

A number of factors seem to have increased overweight. The most prominent are a decline in physical activity, poor diet choices, and (for adults) a decrease in smoking.[13] Most experts also believe that a good, if not the best, preventive approach is to develop more healthy habits among children and adolescents. Although many individual WIC agencies and staffers work hard to combat overweight among WIC participants, a more sustained focus would require adding the prevention of overweight to WIC's mission.

Right now, despite the efforts of many individual WIC agencies and staffers, the total program is largely irrelevant to those concerns. Former Agriculture Secretary Dan Glickman observed:

Currently, for example, there's nothing in the WIC program that says anything about physical activity, even though this is the [number one] reason for the rapid rise in childhood obesity. Through WIC, we encourage parents to stop smoking, to get their children immunized, to eat healthy. We also should encourage active lifestyles. I've asked Shirley [undersecretary for food and nutrition and consumer services] and her staff to take a formal look at all our nutrition programs to see if there's a way to link diet and exercise and address the whole problem, instead of simply the food angle.[14]

Shifting WIC's focus will be no simple matter. Researchers at the Centers for Disease Control, concerned about the increasing prevalence of overweight among four- to five-year-old children, emphasized the importance of prevention activities in the preschool years, such as "encourag[ing] physical activity to maintain a healthy weight, eating at least five servings of fruits and vegetables per day, and after the age of 2 years gradually decreasing dietary fat to a level of no more than 30% of energy."[15] But those are the very ages when WIC participation drops off sharply.

Not only will counseling need to be expanded and reoriented, but the very foundation of the program may have to be reconsidered. That will be a tricky tradeoff. A major reason mothers participate in WIC is to receive the food package. The package, however, is designed to encourage consumption, albeit more healthy consumption. Deny them the package, or make it less attractive, and participation in the children's program may fall off even more.

Serve Children over Age Four?

Current rules cut off WIC eligibility when a child reaches age five. Nutritional needs may change as children mature, but they do not end—in fact, with regard to overweight, they increase. As described above, over the past three decades, the degree of overweight among children and adolescents has steadily increased, and that condition is associated with later overweight and various health problems in adulthood.[16]

Many researchers believe that school-age children should receive nutritional counseling because, as Isobel Contento concluded:

> [B]ehaviors, or the predispositions and skills to enact them are important, . . . and chronic disease processes begin early. Risk factors for chronic disease tend to begin in youth, so that those at the high end in terms of total cholesterol, blood pressure, or weight maintain their ranking in relationship to their peers over time.[17]

Why not have WIC provide that counseling and education? WIC's age cutoff is usually defended on the grounds that school meals programs already address the needs of school-age children. But those programs are designed to increase food consumption, when the problem for many children is excessive consumption—or consumption of the wrong foods. In fact, to address that serious problem, policymakers have developed various programs for specific communities.

The Nutrition in a Changing World program, for example, is for children from kindergarten through grade twelve. Its curriculum focuses on teaching the connection between nutrition and health at lower grades and adds special topics for older students, such as weight control. The Nutrition for Life program is for junior high school students. It has a curriculum related to nutrition that is taught as part of health classes. Children and Adolescent Trial for Cardiovascular Health has a classroom education component that introduces changes in the school environment, including physical activity and school meals. The Gimme 5 program is designed to help fourth and fifth graders "ask for and prepare fruits and vegetables." The San Diego Family Heart Project consists of three months of weekly education sessions—followed by nine months of bimonthly sessions—for both parents and their children and includes social time with healthy snacks. The Nutrition for a Lifetime Study provides an interactive computer video disk in grocery stores that is targeted to children between ages eight and sixteen. The Great Sensations Study consists of classroom instruction combined with a schoolwide media campaign to reduce the consumption of salty snacks among high school students. The Heart Smart Program consists of classroom instruction, cardiovascular screening, and parent and family outreach for fourth and fifth graders at risk of cardiovascular disease.[18]

Allow States to Experiment with Serving Children over Age Four. Why not engage the energies and resources of WIC for such an effort? Rather than continue to raise income limits, policymakers should consider keeping poor children in the program longer. Not only will those over the age of four benefit, but so might three- and four-year-old children, if additional efforts were made to make the program more relevant to their needs.

Longer participation in the WIC program might make it more effective in meeting its basic objectives. As noted above, the National WIC Evaluation found that the dietary status of past WIC participants was no different from the comparison group that did not receive WIC benefits. In other words, not only does the food package end, but the lessons of WIC apparently did not make a permanent change in parental behavior or the child's eating habits. More time in the program might make a more lasting impression, and, even if not, dietary behavior would at least be better for a longer period of time.

Increase Directive Counseling?

WIC is largely "based on the knowledge-attitudes-practice paradigm," according to Schiller and Fox.[19] In fact, as we have noted, parents cannot even be required to attend WIC's basic nutritional counseling sessions, although some may not know that.

A review of the research on nutrition education programs, including WIC, suggests that such programs "were not very effective in bringing about behavioral change" and that "the use of a systematic behavioral change process is most likely to be effective in bringing about changes in behavior."[20] That suggests changing the paradigm used by WIC from providing information to motivating changed behaviors. Schiller and Fox reported:

Effective programs are: behaviorally focused; based on appropriate theory and prior research; interactive; aimed at facilitating voluntary adoption of desired behaviors; and based on identified needs, perceptions, motivations and desires of the target audience.[21]

A group of projects funded by the Centers for Disease Control suggests how much WIC might be able to change parental behavior. In New York City six volunteer WIC sites were randomly assigned to one of three immunization interventions designed to increase vaccination coverage among preschool children who were eligible for measles vaccination.[22] In two sites WIC parents were escorted to a clinic in the same location, where children could be immunized in an "express lane"; in two other sites parents were required to return monthly for WIC coupons, rather than every two months (the normal schedule), until they had the child immunized; and in the final two sites parents were offered a vaccination assessment and education and referral services ordinarily offered in the WIC office. The children at the escort sites were five times more likely to be immunized than children at the referral sites. Similarly, the children at the sites where parents could be required to return each month for their coupons were three times more likely to be immunized. In short, WIC benefits have been used to change recipient behavior for the better.

Federal rules prohibit tying WIC benefits to the acceptance of nutritional instruction or engaging in any other specific behavior. Pregnant smokers cannot even be required to attend smoking-cessation classes, despite the well-known connection between smoking and low birthweight and other adverse birth outcomes. And yet, to the extent that WIC was actually successful in the early studies described above, one explanation could be the nutritional and health counseling that pregnant mothers receive (however inadequate it may now seem), especially given the relatively small size of the food package for all but newborns. And that may be the result of the directive or authoritative content of WIC's counseling. Remember, if the program staff determines that recipients suffer from high cholesterol, it can issue vouchers that can be used only for low-fat foods.

Allow WIC Counseling to Be More Directive. WIC participants could be required to attend life-skills-training and parenting classes as a condition of receiving their food voucher. Smokers could be required to attend smoking-cessation classes. Participants could be required to have

Nurse Home Visitation

The Prenatal and Early Childhood Nurse Home Visitation Program is a highly structured program that uses an authoritative or directive approach to counseling low-income, first-time mothers. (Participation is voluntary.) Nurse home visits begin during pregnancy and continue for two years after the child is born. The nurse home visitors provide a comprehensive set of services that focus on a mother's personal health and development—including services to prevent unintended pregnancy and find employment—and the quality of care giving for the child. As opposed to interventions that are nonjudgmental, the nurse home visitation projects deliver clear behavioral messages by public health nurses. For example, as the *Washington Post* reported, the traditional way of providing family planning would be to say, "If you want to avoid a second baby, here's a condom and how to use it." The authoritative approach is to say, "You shouldn't have another baby and here are ways to prevent it."

A randomized experiment in Elmira, New York, found that the nurse home visitors achieved a 25 percent drop in pregnant women's smoking by the end of the pregnancy, a 75 percent reduction in premature births among pregnant women who had smoked, and large birthweight increases for babies born to young teen mothers—nearly 400 grams for mothers aged 14 to 16. In addition, fifteen-year follow-up findings indicated almost a 31 percent reduction in the subsequent childbearing for low-income, unmarried mothers (1.1 versus 1.6 subsequent births). Verified cases of child abuse and neglect were 79 percent lower, drug and alcohol problems 44 percent lower, arrests among the mothers 69 percent lower, and welfare use 33 percent lower. The reduction in subsequent births was particularly noteworthy, given the apparent failure of other social interventions aimed at addressing that problem. As a result, the program led to large savings in government spending. (Program replications of this study have show similarly impressive results in Memphis, Tennessee, and Denver, Colorado.)

Source: Olds et al. (1997).

their children immunized, perhaps along the lines of the immunization projects described above.

States could be permitted to experiment with such behavior-related rules in the same way they can now condition welfare on specific behaviors.[23] With notable successes, many states have imposed various behavioral rules on their welfare caseloads, such as requiring parents to send their children to school[24] and to immunize them[25] as well as to attend parenting classes. Similar requirements might bring about improved outcomes for WIC participants.

Another possible approach would be to test, on a large-scale basis, an intensive nurse home visitation program. Some WIC agencies have performed limited home visiting; they often used paraprofessionals funded by other programs. The most promising of those programs is the Prenatal and Early Childhood Nurse Home Visitation Program developed by David Olds.[26] (See the sidebar.) WIC recipients could be assigned to either WIC or WIC plus the home visitation program. Although the two programs would share some of the same services and objectives, and both groups would receive WIC food vouchers, their approach to counseling would be quite different. A comparison of outcomes would suggest which program orientation is more effective. Since the home visitation could be considered an enhanced version of WIC's counseling component, the ethical issue of withholding benefits does not arise.

Try Alternative Service Providers?

WIC is a program of the USDA, in keeping with its focus on nutrition services. But WIC works through state health departments, which in turn fund local health departments, hospitals, public health clinics, community health centers, and so forth. Whaley and True recommended that WIC should "investigate collaborations with other health providers to establish more integrated nutrition and health services for low-income families."[27]

WIC was conceived in the early 1970s, long before expansion of various health services for low-income families. Any number of other health care providers might be appropriate WIC agencies. In three states (California, Illinois, and Oklahoma), for example, Planned Parenthood organizations also serve as the local WIC agency.[28]

One way to coordinate health services with WIC is to collocate WIC services with a managed care provider, a measure made easier now by the proliferation of Medicaid managed care. Alan Kendal of Emory University identified five states where at least one WIC agency has collocated WIC services with managed care providers (California, Florida, Michigan, Texas, and Washington). His research in Michigan suggested that collocation can achieve notable improvements in health indicators.[29]

Another approach that merits serious consideration would be to integrate WIC into the actual operations of Medicaid managed care systems. WIC went into effect before Medicaid coverage was expanded to include, among others, the same people covered by WIC—and long before most Medicaid recipients were enrolled in managed care programs. Allowing managed care agencies to provide WIC services might avoid costly duplication of administrative services and would make it easier for WIC participants to avail themselves of the services WIC now refers them to, such as prenatal care. One obstacle to full integration is an almost total prohibition, contained in federal law and regulations, against having for-profit organizations, such as for-profit HMOs, serve as WIC agencies.

Managed care providers might eagerly accept adding WIC services to their own programs—especially if they were to receive additional funding. Offering such WIC-like services could have a positive impact on pregnancy and child outcomes. An Urban Institute study reported that in "at least a couple of states managed care plans and private physicians have already asked about offering WIC services in their offices."[30]

We should, nevertheless, be mindful that managed care plans have been criticized for neglecting preventive activities. Plans and providers who believe that a substantial portion of their clients will shift to other plans before the long-term costs of failing to provide preventive services are realized will be tempted to skimp on them. Hence, any integration of WIC with managed care should be pursued with caution.

Other agencies also share common goals with WIC. For example, in many communities, WIC and Head Start serve the same families. Some have suggested a closer integration of those programs to minimize duplication and maximize program impact. Thus, Whaley and True wrote that "WIC is in an excellent position to go beyond screening and referrals, and actually serve the physical and administrative 'home' for a wide variety of . . . family services."[31]

8

Rigorous Evaluation

Although the foregoing ideas seem consistent with research findings and common sense, they are untried and therefore should be carefully evaluated. Too many social programs are launched and policies changed without a full understanding of the problems they seek to address and without a rigorous evaluation of whether they succeed. Policymakers should systematically explore what might strengthen the program, expand those programmatic elements that work, and discard those that do not.

Given the relatively small effects of the total program, evaluations of program impact should devote more attention to examining the effects on subgroups and components of the program. Such an examination would help policymakers target benefits to the groups that are most helped by the intervention. In other areas of social intervention, the most exciting findings are often for discrete and important subgroups. For example, the positive effects of the Elmira nurse home visitation program, described in chapter 7, were primarily limited to economically disadvantaged mothers, with few significant impacts for the sample as a whole.[1] Similarly, Ohio's Learning, Earning, and Parenting program, an initiative providing financial incentives for teen parents to enroll and attend school, did not have a statistically significant effect on high school graduation or receipt of a general equivalency diploma for teen welfare mothers overall, but it did increase the effect by 18 percent for those who were still in school at the time the project started.[2]

The Limits of Nonexperimental Studies

Although we believe that most WIC researchers have been sincere in their efforts to discern WIC's impacts, the plain fact is that methodological problems (like selection and simultaneity bias) undercut their findings—and make their studies too unreliable for policymaking. As Michael Puma and his Abt Associates colleagues warned, "[T]he risks inherent in the quasi-experimental design" are "results that are either obviously incorrect or, if plausible, subject to grave suspicion."[3] Even in the absence of the state-based experimentation proposed above, the U.S. Department of Agriculture should mount a systematic research effort to determine WIC's impacts.

We should not dismiss nonexperimental studies out of hand. Often they provide the only objective information available about a program's impact. But their findings are extremely difficult to assess when key statistical tests to determine the validity of their findings are not performed or reported fully enough to make a judgment. Hence, nonexperimental studies should pay much more attention to methodological problems such as those identified in this volume. Doing so means testing a range of control variables and instruments, conducting the necessary tests to determine the strength of the instruments, and examining various specifications of the underlying statistical model.

Regrettably, most WIC studies simply do not provide sufficient information with which to judge the strength of their instruments and the adequacy of their statistical models. We note the recurrent problems of omitted variables (that is, limited or poorly crafted control variables that do not capture enough data about the participants) and inadequate instruments (that is, the absence of variables that explain program participation independent of factors that affect the outcomes of interest).[4]

Greater attention to methodological rigor, however, would not necessarily result in more reliable estimates of WIC's impact. The findings of any nonexperimental study are sensitive to the sample selected, the variables considered, and the statistical models used. In addition, subgroup analysis is often complicated by the apparent differential impact of instrumental variables and other methods of controlling for selection effects.

As an illustration, consider the analyses performed by Michael J. Brien and Christopher A. Swann.[5] They used the 1988 National Maternal and Infant Health Survey to estimate the impact of WIC on blacks and whites. They estimated WIC's impact by varying the criteria used to select the sample, the variables included in the statistical model, and the approach to correcting for selection bias. Their research was grounded in sound theory and recognized evaluation methods, but with each modification, the findings fluctuated, sometimes considerably. For example, tables 5-1 and 5-2 summarize their 1999 findings from eight different models.

The estimated impacts on birthweight ranged from −248 grams to 82 grams for whites and from 146 grams to 393 grams for blacks. Some findings were statistically significant, and others were not. Even larger variations were found with respect to the estimated impacts on the incidence of low birthweight; those variations ranged from −6 percent to (a highly implausible) 181 percent for whites and −29 percent to −55 percent for blacks. Thus, even in that very careful work, a great deal of uncertainty remains. (We describe their analyses in detail in the appendix.)

Indeed, randomized experiments may be the only way to develop valid estimates of WIC's impact, because they ordinarily do not require uncertain statistical adjustments to eliminate differences between treatment and control groups. As we and Peter H. Rossi noted:

> If properly planned and implemented, an experimental design should result in treatment and control groups that have comparable measurable and unmeasurable aggregate characteristics (within the limits of chance variation). And, from the moment of randomization, they will be exposed to the same outside forces, such as economic conditions, social environments, and other events—allowing any subsequent differences in average outcomes to be attributed to the intervention.[6]

The need for randomized experiments is becoming increasingly clear to policymakers. Random assignment was the method of choice for measuring the impact of dozens of welfare reform experiments that eventually led to the passage of the 1996 welfare reform law. It also was the strategy recommended by the General Accounting Office in its 1997 review of the Head Start program,[7] in which the GAO outlined a strategy similar to the one we propose here.

Randomized Experiments

As described above, many policymakers assume that it is not ethically appropriate to conduct randomized experiments in the WIC program because such high percentages of eligible recipients already are enrolled. Room for ethical experimentation does, however, exist.

Random Assignment for the Children's Program. In the early 1990s, the USDA solicited proposals for a large-scale experiment designed to measure WIC's impact on children's nutritional status, cognitive development, and other outcomes. In 1992, however, Congress explicitly prohibited the USDA from undertaking the study. Because many advocates felt that the battle for full funding had been won, they may have felt that such a study was unnecessary and could only cause mischief. (After all, a rigorous evaluation of the children's portion of the program might reveal that impacts fall short of the advocates' rhetoric.) The study's $20 million price tag also may have contributed to its demise. Unlike studies of the prenatal portion of WIC, which can rely on relatively inexpensive data sources, such as birth certificates and administrative records, data on children's long-term physical and cognitive development are expensive to collect.

As recently as 1994, researchers at the Urban Institute noted that the lack of evidence regarding WIC's impact on children is a serious problem and argued that a rigorous evaluation should be initiated before substantially more children are added to the program:

> More research is needed on the effect of WIC participation for children, given that this is the group that will grow most under full funding. If we want to learn more about WIC's effects for children, it is important to initiate a study very soon. If full funding is attained, researchers will be unable to identify what WIC does and does not achieve for children, since there will be no control group of comparable nonparticipating children.[8]

It is still possible to initiate a straightforward randomized experiment for children—because they are not yet fully covered by WIC. In 1997, WIC's coverage of children was just 75 percent of those who were eligible.[9] Coverage is even lower for the children in the upper end of that age group.[10] Thus, it might be possible to randomly assign three- and four-year-olds, because the participation of eligible children is still relatively low. The GAO recommended a similar strategy for Head Start in a recent study:

> Randomized trials, however, could be appropriately applied to Head Start research. In fact, the evaluation of the Early Head Start project, now under way, has randomly assigned potential participants to Early Head Start or a control group that has not received Early Head Start services.[11]

More recently, the Advisory Committee on Head Start Research and Evaluation recommended a similar strategy and concluded that "the most rigorous methodological approach to answering questions about impact is to compare children and families who are randomly assigned to Head Start with children and families who are assigned to a control group that does not receive Head Start."[12]

Because WIC has reached full coverage among infants and pregnant,[13] breastfeeding, and postpartum women, it is generally assumed that a randomized experiment for those groups would be unethical to undertake—because some people would be denied a service or a benefit to which they would otherwise be legally entitled. But with a little creativity, it should still be possible to mount a number of ethical randomized experiments.

Random Assignment to Those at the "Policy Margin." One way to obviate concerns about denying benefits to eligible people would be to study WIC's impact on those who are not now eligible—but who are, in important ways, similar to those who are. For example, the experiment could involve families with incomes just over income eligibility or children just over age four. Such experiments could be conducted, for example, in the states that have not availed themselves of the option to expand Medicaid to children with family incomes above 185 percent of poverty.

Although it would be technically incorrect to apply findings from such studies to all WIC recipients, the results would be suggestive about the current program's impact and highly suggestive concerning those at the upper edges of eligibility. More important, the results would inform policymakers about the wisdom or direction of continued expansions of the program to those at the "policy margin."

Such studies could be complex, randomized experiments in which impacts are measured across various expansions in eligibility. For example, if no significant improvements were observed by extending WIC to higher-income children, but measurable improvements resulted from extending it to five-year-olds, a reconsideration of the program's target groups would be in order. It might then make sense to experiment further by testing the impact of reducing the income thresholds while raising the age limit for children's eligibility.

Random Assignment to Dose-Response and Planned-Variation Studies. Assuming that WIC produces positive outcomes, it is unclear which of its benefits or services are responsible. Rossi cautioned:

Although the effects of WIC have been attributed to the dietary supplements, they are more properly viewed as the joint effects of the supplements, WIC administration, and WIC nutrition education. Because all WIC participants get all three, the effects of each cannot be estimated separately.[14]

Increasing WIC's impact is best accomplished with a knowledge of which of its elements seem to have the greatest effect on recipients. That knowledge would help determine whether the intensity of the entire program should be increased or only some element of it, such as the food packages or the nutritional counseling.

Randomly assigning people to WIC and to what could be characterized as enhanced versions of WIC would also obviate the ethical dilemma of denying services to eligible populations. Such randomized trials would indirectly measure WIC's effectiveness while assessing the utility and impact of various program enhancements.

Experimental designs could be used to compare the impact of WIC's nutrition education and counseling services with a more comprehensive and aggressive intervention to improve the dietary intake of participants and to modify known risk behaviors such as smoking and substance abuse. Or there could be experiments with increasing the size or value of the food package—or replacing the WIC voucher with cash. A cash-out experiment could examine the extent to which the current WIC food voucher actually increases food consumption and nutrient intake relative to a cash transfer.

The GAO's 1997 review of the Head Start program also suggested this approach to randomized experimentation:

> Another strategy that could be used to study specific parts of the program would be to use an alternative treatment design. In this case, some randomly assigned participants would receive the full Head Start program, while others would receive partial services. For example, if the study interest is in school and cognitive issues, the control group might receive only nutritional and health services.[15]

Unlike the GAO, however, we recommend that the regular WIC program be compared with an enhanced version, rather than with one offering partial services. One exception to that rule could be experiments involving those currently not eligible for the program, such as children age five and older. Such an experiment would involve an expansion of services for them.

Random Assignment to Alternative Health-Related Service Providers. Finally, varying the provider of services poses no ethical problem. For the reasons described above, we believe that other service providers might be more effective in achieving WIC's goals. Experimental designs could be used to test the relative efficacy of various health-related or family service providers. Furthermore, if large enough, the experiment could also involve a variation in services provided.

We do not mean to suggest that randomized experiments would be easy to carry out. Such studies often present daunting organizational and implementation problems. Even when ethical issues are overcome, randomization can create hostility among service staff and impede successful implementation. Larry Orr of Abt Associates described how random assignment appears to have been compromised in one WIC evaluation by program staff, who viewed denying WIC benefits as unacceptable:

> [I]n a pilot test of an evaluation of the [WIC program], local staff recruited women in health clinic waiting rooms and randomly assigned them on the spot, using an algorithm based on the women's Social Security number. Proper application of the algorithm would have produced equally sized treatment and control groups. In one site, nearly two-thirds of women were assigned to the treatment group; it seems clear that recruiters falsified Social Security numbers to allow women who should have been controls to be assigned to the program.[16]

9

Conclusion

Our analysis of the research on WIC's value challenges the conventional wisdom that it is a uniquely successful program. In all probability, many WIC recipients benefit, even if only modestly, from its combination of food packages and counseling services. As we have seen, however, many claims about WIC's effectiveness are simply misleading exaggerations. Moreover, the WIC program as a whole would likely fail a benefit-cost test.

Some observers have argued that the weaknesses in WIC research (and presumably WIC as well) should not be discussed, lest public and political support for the program be undermined. But unless WIC is assessed honestly, the program can never be effectively improved. Would that not hurt poor children even more?

Conversely, WIC provides what could be important benefits to more than 7 million people. In many inner-city neighborhoods, the program's $100 worth of food has become an important component of the economic safety net for mothers with newborns. In addition, we admit to being moved by the testimony of frontline health care workers who describe the importance of WIC packages for newborns.[1]

Clearly, restraint and sensibility are called for. But sensibility is not the same as inaction.

Appendix:
Attempting to Correct
for Selection Bias

Two studies by Michael J. Brien and Christopher A. Swann, former colleagues at the University of Virginia, have demonstrated how sensitive WIC's impacts can be to decisions regarding sample selection, control variables, and the specification of statistical models.[1] (See tables 5-1 and 5-2.) Their research is perhaps the most extensive effort undertaken to address the problem of selection bias in estimating the impact of WIC on birth outcomes. Despite the care with which they approached the problem, however, their research did not produce a consistent set of estimates regarding WIC's effects. On the contrary, their research led to even greater uncertainty. As Peter H. Rossi concluded after reading the research, "Truth about WIC is still elusive."[2]

Brien and Swann's first study was conducted in 1997, while Swann was at Mathematica Policy Research.[3] Like Anne R. Gordon and Lyle Nelson, they used data from the live-birth sample of the 1988 National Maternal and Infant Health Survey, which contains information on the characteristics and experiences of women who had a live birth in 1988. Unlike Gordon and Nelson, however, they restricted their sample to non-Hispanic whites and non-Hispanic blacks "because of known differences between these groups."[4] They selected WIC participants (the treatment group) and eligible nonparticipants (the comparison group) if they had family incomes below 185 percent of the poverty guidelines and if they were at nutritional risk as measured by certain criteria in the

National Maternal and Infant Health Survey. Those criteria included having a prior poor pregnancy outcome; being obese or thin for height; using tobacco, alcohol, or drugs within the three-month period of knowing of the pregnancy; conceiving frequently; or being under the age of nineteen or over the age of thirty-four at the time of conception.

Brien and Swann's second study, conducted in 1999, was essentially another try at what they attempted in their first one, but it had several modifications.[5] First, they added the infant death sample to the live birth sample of the National Maternal and Infant Health Survey. In addition, they altered the eligibility criteria by using a higher income threshold (250 percent of poverty versus 185 percent of poverty) and by dropping the nutritional risk criteria from the sample-selection process. They raised the income threshold, because the survey's income measure is an imperfect proxy for WIC eligibility and using the lower 185 percent standard was found to exclude a considerable number of WIC participants and eligible nonparticipants from the analysis.[6] They dropped the nutritional risk criteria because "discussions with WIC experts suggested that the risk factors used by the program were fairly general and not that binding."[7] Moreover, the data set did not allow them to replicate the nutritional risk factors used by the program. Finally, they added a more comprehensive list of variables to model the WIC participation decision (that is, instruments) by using data from a survey of state WIC agencies that provided details on how individual states administer the program. As we shall see, those choices appear to have a modest influence on the estimated impacts.[8]

Brien and Swann's 1997 study began by estimating WIC's impact on birthweight by using a basic ordinary least squares model, with "a set of biological variables, indicators for the education level of the mother, and indicators for geographic region." The results of that "basic" model indicated that for blacks, WIC increased birthweight by 4.8 percent and reduced the incidence of low-birthweight babies by 39 percent. For whites, birthweight increased 1.6 percent, and incidence of low birthweight fell 3 percent, but neither result was statistically significant. The 1999 study used a similar model but included the expanded data set. That study found that for blacks, WIC increased birthweight by 5.6 percent and reduced the incidence of low-birthweight babies by 40 percent. For whites, birthweight increased 1 percent, and the incidence of low birthweight increased 3 percent, but neither finding was statistically significant.

The basic model in both studies suggested that WIC has positive effects for blacks but has no discernible effects for whites. In response to a personal communication, Brien and Swann estimated the impact of WIC by "using a pooled sample of whites and blacks." Their findings suggest that WIC increased birthweight by 2.3 percent, but after controlling for selection bias by using two-stage least squares, that effect became negative (–.4 percent) and statistically insignificant.[9]

In both studies, Brien and Swann tested a number of alternative specifications to their "basic" model, including other demographic, socioeconomic, and behavioral variables that may affect birthweight. They did not include those variables in their basic model because of concerns of potential "endogeneity" of the variables. The authors explained, for example, that whether the mother smokes or drinks during pregnancy can affect birthweight, but women undertaking those activities also may make other decisions that lead to lower-birthweight babies. In their 1997 study, incorporating additional demographic, socioeconomic, and behavioral variables reduced the birthweight estimate for blacks to 3.8 percent and the incidence in low birthweight to 28 percent.[10] Those changes, however, had the opposite effect for whites; the estimated increase in birthweight rose from a statistically insignificant 1.6 percent to a statistically significant 2.7 percent. The impact on the incidence of low birthweight remained statistically insignificant (–2 percent), however.

In their 1999 study, Brien and Swann refined their variations to their "basic" model. First, they added only demographic and socioeconomic variables to their model, which increased effects for blacks from 5.6 percent to 6 percent.[11] They then added behavioral variables, which reduced the impact to 4.7 percent.[12] (Their estimates on changes in the incidence of low birthweight improved from a reduction of 40 percent to a reduction of 41 percent but then fell back to a reduction of 29 percent when the behavioral variables were added.) For whites, the same modifications increased estimated birthweight effects from a statistically insignificant 1 percent to 2 percent and 2.4 percent, respectively. (The estimated reductions in the incidence of low birthweight remained small and statistically insignificant at –3 percent and –6 percent, respectively.)

Brien and Swann then attempted to correct for selection bias by using a variety of state-level instruments reflecting the generosity and availability of the WIC program in each state, which in turn may affect the chances of program participation.[13] Those variables included state eligibility policies related to the self-declaration of income and use of income allowances or exemptions, the imposition of brand restrictions on food that can be purchased, the use of Aid to Families with Dependent Children eligibility for WIC eligibility, and the first trimester hemoglobin cutoff used for nutritional risk determinations. Other variables used included the number of WIC clinics per 1,000 poor people, the number of WIC clinics per 1,000 square miles in the state, and the generosity of each state's welfare benefits. The 1997 and 1999 studies had slight differences in the choice of instruments used. The authors found that those instruments were better predictors of WIC participation for blacks than for whites.

Brien and Swann then used two-stage least squares to correct for selection bias, an approach equivalent to the instrumental variables method used by Gordon and Nelson. In their 1997 study, that correction increased the birthweight impacts for blacks to 13.6, but the effect on the incidence of low birthweight was no longer statistically significant. Brien and Swann cautioned, however, that those corrections were sensitive to the choice of instruments. The authors then reestimated their equations by excluding various variables from their set of instruments. The birthweight results remained high, at 13.2 percent, and the effect on the incidence of low birthweight remained statistically insignificant. For whites, those modifications increased the point estimates to 5.3 percent and 6.8 percent, but they were not statistically significant. Similarly, the incidence of low-birthweight findings remained statistically insignificant.

In the 1999 study, that approach resulted in birthweight effects for blacks of 9.5 percent, and the estimated effect on the incidence of low birthweight increased to –58 percent, although that was no longer statistically significant. For whites, however, the researchers found that WIC *reduced* birthweight by 4.5 percent and *increased* the incidence of low birthweight by 47 percent, although neither estimate was statistically significant. Again, Brien and Swann cautioned that those corrections were sensitive to the choice of instruments. They then reestimated their equations by excluding various variables from their set of instruments. The findings for blacks were sensitive to the model used, as birthweight impacts ranged from 6.3 percent to 12.7 percent, although the latter was the only statistically significant finding. The findings on reductions in the incidence of low birthweight fell within the range of –45 percent to –55 percent, but none were statistically significant. For whites, the birthweight results remained statistically insignificant for whites, but the point estimates ranged from *reductions* in birthweight of .7 percent to 7.3 percent. Again, their findings suggested that WIC *increased* the incidence of low birthweight from as little as 16 percent to as much as 181 percent, with the latter being the only finding that was statistically significant.

Brien and Swann expressed some concern that the instruments might not do well in predicting WIC participation. They therefore used a second approach for correcting for selection bias by controlling for "maternal fixed effects." The "fixed-effects" method is built on the assumption that differences in birthweight and other birth outcomes are from a mother-specific effect, such as motivation, that remains constant over time. If the mother participated in WIC during one pregnancy but not another, then comparing the birth outcomes from the pregnancy in which she participated in WIC with the one in which she did not gives a measure of WIC's effects. Thus, the analysis requires looking at mothers who have two or more live births with at least one live birth occurring before 1988 and at whether changes in WIC participation status (that is, participating in WIC during one pregnancy but not another) result in differences in birth outcomes.[14] The problem with such an approach is that the mother-specific effect may not be fixed over time. Moreover, considering the findings to be representative of the WIC program requires an assumption that mothers with two or more live births are not systematically different from mothers with only one birth. Brien explained that the exclusion of women with only one birth can affect the interpretation of the findings. He noted that doing so

> depends on how different women with multiple births are [from] the population of all women with a child. On the one hand, women with more than one birth may be more likely to have experienced a favorable birth outcome. On the other, many women with one birth will eventually have two or more births.[15]

In each study, the sample consisted of more than 6,250 pairs of births for white and black women. In using that approach, the difference in birth outcomes between the two pregnancies was the dependent variable, and the independent variables were differences in control variables. Those variables included changes in smoking behavior, the sex of the child, and an indicator for whether the woman had had a marriage between the pregnancies. Unfortunately, the National Maternal and Infant Health Survey does not contain as much information on prior births as it does on births in 1988, and thus it limits the control variables available. The WIC variable was "an indicator that equals one if the mother switches from nonparticipation to participation, minus one if she switches from participation to nonparticipation, and zero otherwise."

In their 1997 study, that approach led to results for blacks that were statistically significant but considerably smaller than found when using two-stage least squares. The increase in birthweight was 4.9 percent. Unlike many of the earlier specifications, however, the findings with respect to the incidence of low birthweight were statistically significant, with a reduction of 4.2 percentage points, or about 30 percent.[16] The findings from the 1999 study were nearly identical, with an increase in birthweight of just 4.8 percent and a reduction in the incidence of low birthweight of 4.5 percentage points, or about 33 percent. The results for whites were small and statistically insignificant.

Brien and Swann offered some possible explanations for the finding that WIC might have beneficial effects for blacks, but not for whites:

> First, it may be the case that prior to any WIC intervention, white mothers are, in unobserved ways, healthier at the time of their pregnancy. The marginal impact of WIC may therefore be smaller for this group. . . . A related explanation for the racial differences may lie in racial differences in the risk factors that result in WIC eligibility. . . . It may be the case, for example, that the program is effective in reducing the incidence of nutritional deficiencies such as anemia among recipients but not the incidence of smoking or drug use. If this is true and if black women are more likely to suffer from nutritional deficiencies and white women are more likely to be eligible because of substance abuse, then the program will have a larger effect for black women than white women. . . . An additional explanation for the racial differences may be related to the participation in other welfare programs. . . . It is possible that what appear to be beneficial effects of WIC participation for blacks are really beneficial effects of multiple program participation. If this is true, then our estimate of WIC participation overstates the true effect.[17]

Of course, race is likely a proxy for various unmeasured factors among participants or programs—for example, age and marital status at first birth, extreme poverty, or social disorganization. But without greater certainty about the underlying findings, such speculation is just that—speculation.

Commentaries

10

Addressing the Selection-Bias Problem for Program Targeting and Design

Michael J. Brien and Christopher A. Swann

In part 1, "Rethinking WIC," Douglas J. Besharov and Peter Germanis provide a comprehensive look at the WIC program. They attempt to summarize the existing literature, including our own, to gain some understanding about what does and does not work. They correctly point out that precisely estimating the effects of WIC participation on a number of important outcomes is difficult for a variety of reasons, the most important of which may be selection bias.[1]

We strongly agree with Besharov and Germanis that it is important to understand whether WIC, a politically popular program that served more than 7 million participants in 1998, works and for whom. Over the past thirty years, federal welfare policy has undergone many changes and is moving increasingly in the direction of providing in-kind benefits rather than cash. Changes include, for example, the introduction of the Medicaid, food stamp, and WIC programs and the replacement of the Aid to Families with Dependent Children program with the more restrictive Temporary Assistance to Needy Families program. In such an environment it is clearly important to understand whether and how well those programs work. In this chapter we provide our thoughts—based on our recent research—about whether WIC works for different groups and then provide some closing comments on other aspects of the program.

Does WIC Work?

Our discussion focuses on two distinct projects. First, we have recently attempted to estimate the effects of pregnant women's WIC participation on a number of birth outcomes that are of interest to policymakers and social scientists.[2] The impetus for that work was that most previous studies used small samples that were not nationally representative, a technique that limited the generalizability of the results. In addition, no previous work was able to control adequately for selection into the WIC program. Second, in more preliminary work, we have examined whether either the mother's or the child's participation in WIC improves the child's health.[3] The motivation for the project was the lack of evidence about the effect of WIC participation on that large and important group of recipients.

The two projects share a number of important features. First, many studies of the WIC program have focused on women at one clinic, in one county, or in one or a few states; that focus leads to concern about whether the results obtained will generalize to a national population. Generalizability might be a problem if heterogeneity existed across geographic locations in program participants, in those administering the program, or in the level of non-WIC benefits available. In our work, we have used nationally representative data from the National Maternal and Infant Health Survey. The survey contains information on a sample of women who gave birth in 1988. The women were surveyed shortly after the 1988 birth and again in 1991. We used the 1988 data for the birth outcomes study and both the 1988 and 1991 data for the child health study. Although the data are now more than a decade old, they are well suited to investigations involving WIC. The survey collected a significant amount of information about participation in the program during pregnancies, the behavior of the women during those periods, and detailed information on the pregnancy outcomes.

Second, the significant contribution of our work has been our handling of selection bias. Besharov and Germanis are correct when they note that not accounting for selection bias can lead to misleading inferences about the effectiveness of WIC. For the birth outcomes project, we used two different strategies, two-stage least squares and "fixed effects," to deal with selection bias.[4] To use two-stage least squares, we required some variables that helped explain WIC participation but did not explain the birth outcomes under consideration. We used data on state-to-state differences in WIC program rules, the availability of WIC clinics, and the generosity of other related transfer programs. The data on state-level WIC program rules are particularly notable, because our analysis represents the first time—to our knowledge—that the data have been used to explain individual-level decisions to participate in WIC. We constructed the instruments by using data from a 1988 survey of local WIC agencies conducted by the U.S. Department of Agriculture, the federal agency that operates the program. We designed the survey to gain a better understanding of how the program is administered below the federal level. Our analysis of the data revealed that some program rules, such as the ease with which applicants can declare their income, play a statistically significant role in explaining the decision to participate in WIC.

To use the fixed-effects estimator, we assumed that the nonrandom selection into WIC exists because of some unchanging maternal characteristic, for example, poor reproductive health. We considered a sample of women from the National Maternal and Infant Health Survey who had at least one birth before the 1988 birth. If the maternal characteristic is unchanging, taking differences in birthweights of the woman's children will net out the maternal effect. Essentially, we asked whether women who did not participate in WIC during a previous pregnancy but did participate for the 1988 birth experienced increased birthweights and whether women who switched from participating to not participating experienced reduced birthweights.

Birth Outcomes

In the appendix to part 1, Besharov and Germanis suggest that our work on birth outcomes "leads to even greater uncertainty" about the effectiveness of WIC. While we agree that our work has not produced a single set of estimates across all models and all specifications, we believe that our work does show a consistent positive effect for blacks. With the background discussed above, we now briefly consider a small subset of our results for birth outcomes: the effect of WIC on the logarithm of birthweight and the incidence of low birthweight. Estimating our models with ordinary least squares and thus ignoring any selection problem, we found that WIC had an effect on birthweight of between 0 and 2 percent for whites and 4.7 to 6.0 percent for blacks, depending on model specification. We found no effect of WIC on the likelihood of a low birthweight for whites and a reduction of between 3.9 and 5.6 percentage points in the probability of low birthweight for blacks. Thus, the ordinary least squares results consistently demonstrated that WIC was effective for blacks and showed some positive effects for whites, although the results for whites were weaker in both magnitude and statistical significance.

What happened when we controlled for selection? Focusing first on blacks, our two-stage least squares estimates showed that WIC resulted in a *statistically significant* increase in birthweight of almost 10 percent. The effect on the probability of a low birthweight was a statistically insignificant 7.9 percentage points. When we used our fixed-effects estimator, the effect on birthweight was a more modest but still statistically significant 4.8 percent. Furthermore, the model showed a statistically significant reduction of 4.5 percentage points in the probability of a low birthweight.

The results for blacks consistently showed a positive effect for WIC, even after we controlled for selection. The two-stage least squares results were stronger in magnitude and somewhat weaker in statistical significance when compared with the fixed-effects estimator, and they were somewhat sensitive to the choice of instruments. Consistent with the ordinary least squares results, the estimates for whites were weaker. The results after controlling for selection were not statistically significant and were sometimes of the "wrong" sign.

What does all of that mean? Is WIC simply not effective for whites? Is the problem our model or our data? Of course, it is hard to know for sure; WIC may be effective for whites, but our data may simply not show that. As Besharov and Germanis note at the end of their appendix, we had a number of hypotheses for that result. Our hypotheses included racial differences in unobserved health, risk factors for WIC eligibility, and participation rates in other welfare programs, but we did not attempt to test those hypotheses in our 1999 study.[5]

Regardless of the explanation, the difference remains: WIC appears to be effective for blacks but not for whites. We estimated that WIC increases birthweights for black infants by between 4.7 and 9.5 percent. The results suggest that there was adverse selection, whereby women in poorer unobserved health sought out WIC benefits. Furthermore, we estimated that WIC participation reduced the likelihood of a low birthweight by between 3.9 and 7.9 percentage points—although the 7.9 percentage point estimate was not statistically significant.

Child Health

To this point our discussion has focused on only one category of WIC participants—pregnant women. More than three-fourths of the WIC participants, however, are infants and children, and as Besharov and

Germanis point out, the literature in this area is sparse. In preliminary research[6] using the longitudinal follow-up to the National Maternal and Infant Health Survey, we examined the effect of WIC on several measures of child health. As discussed above, we controlled for selection into the WIC program by using two-stage least squares.

We considered three types of outcomes: anthropometric measures such as age-standardized height (a measure of long-term child health) and height-standardized weight (a measure of short-term child health), the physician's assessment of the child's health (from excellent to poor), and the mother's assessment of the child's health (from excellent to poor). For policy variables we considered maternal participation only, the child's participation only, and participation by either the mother or child.

We found no signficant effects of WIC participation on any of the anthropometric measures of child health. We found limited evidence that WIC participation led to better assessments of child health by physicians, but even those results were somewhat sensitive to the particular specification of the model. While those results are preliminary, they suggest that at best only limited evidence exists that WIC participation improves commonly used measures of child health. More work on the topic is clearly warranted.

Can WIC Be More Effective?

Our work suggests that WIC may be more effective for groups of women who are more disadvantaged; thus, targeting benefits to the most disadvantaged women may improve the effectiveness of WIC. For example, using a lower income cutoff or a stricter interpretation of nutritional risk would tighten eligibility requirements and, in effect, focus the resources on the women who are the most in need. Along those lines, it would be interesting to know something about the number of women who are denied WIC benefits and the reason(s) for the denial. Are significant numbers of women turned away because they do not meet the nutritional criteria? Do rates of denial vary significantly by state or region?

We would also like to see agencies granted more flexibility to improvise on the basis of local conditions. It is not immediately obvious that spending a marginal dollar on food has a larger effect than spending that dollar on nutritional counseling. Because WIC clinics are locally based and run, they may in fact be particularly good places to provide counseling. Of course, it may take the lure of food benefits to bring the women into the clinic.

We believe that more research is needed to understand fully the effect of WIC participation on maternal behavior such as smoking and drinking and on child health in broad terms. Additionally, it would be very helpful to gain a better understanding of the decision to participate in WIC and of how that decision interacts with the decision to participate in a host of other programs designed to improve the health and well-being of low-income families.

11

An Incremental Approach to Testing WIC's Efficacy

Nancy R. Burstein

How could anyone possibly be opposed to the WIC program? Not even the strongest advocates of smaller government would question the desirability of spending taxpayer dollars to ensure good birth outcomes and give children a healthy start on life.

But let us play devil's advocate. Suppose that the WIC program has no beneficial effect on participants other than freeing up some of their food budget. The WIC program costs money to administer and may have the deleterious effect of inducing more women to bottle-feed their infants because the program eliminates the cost advantage of breastfeeding. Under that scenario the program is simply a waste of administrative resources. To justify WIC, it is necessary to establish that food vouchers plus nutrition education plus health care referrals have a sufficient effect, beyond that of a simple transfer of cash, to counterbalance the program costs. In my view, although that may indeed be the case, no persuasive empirical evidence exists on either side of the question. Practically speaking, we know no more about the effects of WIC now than before the program was introduced.

Theoretical Evidence on the Effects of WIC

Advocates for WIC have proposed plausible mechanisms through which beneficial effects could occur that correspond to each component of the program. Experience has taught us, however, that the intended effects of a program do not always materialize. For each mechanism, we should consider and assess possible barriers to its realization.

Hypothesis 1. WIC provides nutritious food to low-income pregnant and postpartum women, to infants, and to children who are at nutritional risk and thereby improves their nutritional status.

Against that hypothesis we should consider three ideas. First, "nutritional risk" may not well define a population that requires nutritional assistance. As currently used, the concept includes hardships and disabilities that adversely affect some of the same outcomes that depend on good nutrition but that are not themselves directly related to nutrition, for example, mental retardation, lead poisoning, and exposure to second-hand cigarette smoke. Hence, some people determined by a competent professional authority to be at nutritional risk may not be in especial need of nutritious food.

Second, provision of nutritious foods may fail to improve recipients' nutritional status for several reasons. Recipients may decline to eat some of the WIC foods or may share food with family members. Alternatively, they may already be getting enough of the target nutrients. The main special nutritional needs of the categorically defined WIC populations—excluding infants—are protein and certain micronutrients, for example, calcium and folate. But the diet of virtually all Americans contains far more protein than needed. With regard to micronutrients, nutritional supplements—multivitamin pills—are certainly sufficient and probably necessary for vulnerable populations to attain their dietary goals.

Finally, the most important nutrition-related problem of low-income Americans is obesity, which provision of WIC foods does not address.

Hypothesis 2. WIC provides nutritional education, which improves participants' knowledge and, ultimately, their behavior.

Against that hypothesis we should consider two points. First, WIC is unlikely to improve participants' knowledge substantively, given the voluntary nature of the nutrition-education component and its extremely limited scope. Second, changing people's eating habits usually requires more than changing their knowledge. Looking at other areas of human behavior, we see that many people still smoke cigarettes or engage in unprotected sex, although hardly anyone could be unaware of the potentially fatal risks of doing so.

Hypothesis 3. By providing health care referrals, WIC increases the receipt of prenatal care, well-baby care, and immunizations. That preventive care reduces the occurrence of subsequent serious complications.

Nevertheless, we should consider that many of those who are given referrals might have found their way to health care providers even if there was no explicit linkage. Conversely, not all those who receive referrals from WIC necessarily follow up on them. The extent to which WIC participation increases receipt of preventive care is an empirical question.

In summary, plausible mechanisms indeed exist through which the WIC program could have beneficial effects, but those effects are by no means guaranteed. If those effects do not occur, the program is not worthwhile. It is therefore essential to measure the effects correctly.

Empirical Evidence on the Effects of WIC

As Douglas J. Besharov and Peter Germanis discuss, many researchers have attempted to estimate the impact of WIC participation on outcomes such as birthweight, breastfeeding, and nutrient intake. In my opinion those studies, with a single exception (discussed below), constitute inadmissible evidence because they use comparison group designs, in which the outcomes of WIC participants are compared with the outcomes of income-eligible nonparticipants. That is not to say that randomized studies are always necessary to determine effects of interventions. Simple aggregate time series are sufficient when major effects are expected to occur, for example, when bringing sewer lines into an area with high mortality from waterborne diseases or when installing a traffic light at an intersection that has had many traffic accidents. Even in dramatic cases like those, however, we might be reluctant to rely on a comparison group design without a time-series component because of the likelihood of confounding factors. In evaluating WIC, we have the additional consideration that the expected effects are small.

In assessing studies of WIC, we note the existence of plenty of prima facie evidence that WIC participants would differ from income-eligible nonparticipants on the outcomes of interest, either positively or negatively, even absent the program, and for reasons that are hard to measure. For example, WIC participants are people who are willing to drink milk, eat unsugared cereal, and consume the other components of the WIC food package. In addition, their perceived need is sufficiently long-term that they are willing to go through the application process. Moreover, they have been certified, in many cases, to have conditions that would negatively affect the outcomes of interest and that cannot be "cured" by WIC participation, for example, lead poisoning.

Many other instances can be given of characteristics of WIC participants that practically definitionally distinguish them from comparison groups with respect to expected outcomes absent the program.

In recent years, some authors have attempted to control for selection bias by using sophisticated econometric techniques. One sometimes sees the statement that econometric techniques such as instrumental variables or its variants have corrected for selection bias "to some extent." That is a potentially misleading notion. It suggests that the adjustment has brought the parameter estimate—for example, the impact of WIC on birthweight—closer to the true value than the unadjusted estimate. In fact, the instrumental variables adjustment may well result in an estimate that is farther from the truth than the initial estimate. Evidence on that issue appeared in a classic article by R. LaLonde and R. Maynard,[1] in which they tested various methods that had been proposed to correct for selection bias. The authors reached the dispiriting conclusion that none of those methods yielded impact estimates similar to those that had actually been observed in a randomized experiment. Further evidence of the unreliability of selection bias corrections may be seen in "nonsensical" instrumental variables estimates, which are rejected by their authors because they have the wrong sign. In at least four studies of WIC that used instrumental variables approaches,[2] the authors got unacceptable results—for example, that WIC reduced birthweight—and concluded that the selection bias correction "didn't work" and that the results therefore were not to be believed. Why, then, should results be believed when they show a beneficial effect of WIC? As Anne R. Gordon and Lyle Nelson remarked:

> It is possible that the selection-bias-correction models of the effects of WIC on birth outcomes produce unstable and implausible results because the factors affecting WIC participation and birthweight are very nearly identical, since WIC targets low-income women at risk for poor pregnancy outcomes. In this case, modeling the participation decision is not likely to be a useful approach to controlling for selection bias.[3]

A less dangerous approach appears to me to be single-equation methods that include better measures of treatment group–comparison group differences. Selection bias can be thought of as a problem of omitted variables. If all the differences between participants and eligible nonparticipants could be measured and included in the model, the equation would be correct. Yet, again, a caution is in order: Eliminating some sources of selection bias does not necessarily reduce the net effect of the bias, because the various sources of bias may operate in either direction. The mild advantage that approach has over instrumental variables is that the reader can reason, for example, that the "most important" variables that remain unmeasured in all likelihood would increase (or decrease) the parameter estimate, so that the direction of bias may be inferred. Such inference is not possible with instrumental variables models.

The sole rigorous evaluation of WIC of which I am aware is a study by James Metcoff and others on the impact of WIC on birthweight.[4] That study used a small sample ($n = 410$) of pregnant women entering a prenatal clinic in one hospital in Oklahoma who were randomly assigned to WIC-participant or nonparticipant groups. A significant positive effect on birthweight was found for smokers only. We thus have credible evidence from one small study of a single site that WIC participation by pregnant women increased birthweight among smokers (but not among nonsmokers). Although encouraging, that is not enough to justify a multibillion-dollar program.

Is WIC Working Yet?

We cannot reasonably talk about how to make WIC work better if we do not know whether it is working at all. It may indeed be the most excellent program in the *Federal Register.* But we need some credible evidence that it is effective.

I realize that policymakers deem it unthinkable to perform a rigorous experimental study of WIC that would entail denying WIC services to some eligible participants. That is a mind-set I would like to see changed. History is full of protocols that were deemed unalterable for years at great cost to the affected people. Most recently, the extreme treatment of breast cancer through bone marrow transplant and massive chemotherapy was found to be medically valueless, although extremely expensive and quite painful to the patients.

I have for years advocated an incremental approach to testing the efficacy of WIC. To state this more forcefully than Besharov and Germanis, my proposal is that national demonstrations be conducted consisting of three populations: children age five who are otherwise eligible (that is, under 185 percent of poverty and with identified nutritional risks);

nonbreastfeeding women, seven to twelve months postpartum, who otherwise are eligible; and people in all WIC categories with nutritional risks but with incomes ranging from 185 percent to 250 percent of poverty.

I suggest that we randomly assign people in those categories to three treatment groups: no benefits; participation in WIC; and a novel alternative, *receipt of food stamps equal to the value of the WIC food package,* with no nutrition education or health care referrals. In contrasting the outcomes for the first two groups, we would be learning the answer to the basic question, Does WIC work? In contrasting the outcomes for the last two groups, however, we would be testing the impact of WIC vouchers, nutrition education, and health care referrals *above and beyond* the simple effect of increasing families' ability to buy food. Furthermore, I would want the food stamp benefit offered to infants to be sufficient to buy formula, regardless of the mode of feeding that was chosen. Mothers in the last group would still be able to bottle-feed their infants, but they also would have the option of breastfeeding them and using the stamps to buy other food.[5] Would such an approach increase the prevalence of breastfeeding? Or would some mothers use that flexibility inappropriately to feed their infants cow's milk or some cheaper alternative? We shall not know until we try.

If WIC is shown to have positive effects on those currently ineligible groups, then we may conclude a fortiori that it is effective for the inframarginal populations. But if not, we should have the courage to test WIC in the same way on the margins of the currently eligible populations, which include the following groups: children ages three and four; breastfeeding women seven- to twelve-months postpartum; nonbreastfeeding women zero- to six-months postpartum; people with only dietary risks; and people in all WIC categories with incomes ranging from 130 to 185 percent of poverty.

Those experiments could be of the greatest value to policymakers. Although WIC is not doing serious harm to participants, it may simply be a colossal waste. Or perhaps it is so excellent that it should be expanded even further. The problem is, we do not know. We need to keep an open mind about the effectiveness of such popular but untested programs and start testing them rigorously.

12

A Defense of the Existing Research on WIC

Barbara L. Devaney

In part 1 of this volume, "Rethinking WIC," Douglas J. Besharov and Peter Germanis conduct a detailed and comprehensive review of the WIC program and the research on its effects. They critique the existing research and propose some interesting policy options. Their criticisms fall into two general categories: methodological issues, particularly the limitation presented by selection bias, and gaps in the effectiveness of WIC for different subgroups, most notably children ages one to four.

Many of their criticisms of the WIC research have some validity. In particular, they note correctly that studies of the effectiveness of pregnant women's participation in the WIC program cannot be generalized to studies of the effects on children. In addition, as with all program evaluation, methodological issues are complex and must be considered carefully in drawing conclusions about program effectiveness.

Nonetheless, a substantial body of evidence exists on the effectiveness of WIC. To be sure, the methodological limitations raised by Besharov and Germanis must affect our understanding of the exact effects of WIC. In attempting to correct what they perceive as an exaggeration of WIC's effects, however, Besharov and Germanis may, in fact, swing to the opposite extreme and downplay some important evidence on the role of WIC.

The following discussion first focuses on the Besharov and Germanis critique of the research and its implications, goes on to provide a brief summary of what we do know about the effectiveness of WIC, and then considers some of Besharov and Germanis's proposed policy alternatives.

What Is Selection Bias, and How Does It Affect What We Know about WIC?

One of the main criticisms of the WIC literature centers on the use of a quasi-experimental methodology to examine WIC effects and the resulting potential for selection bias to affect estimated program effects. The pervasive point in their critique is the potential for selection bias to undermine, rather than to limit or even inform, the studies of WIC effectiveness. The implicit conclusion that selection bias undermines the research studies overstates the limitations of the research on the effectiveness of WIC.

The "gold standard" for evaluating government programs and policies is a randomized design, whereby eligible applicants are randomly assigned to either a program group that receives benefits or a control group that does not. Because the two groups are formed randomly, differences in outcomes between the two groups are the best measure of program effects. Random-assignment designs, however, have the major disadvantage of denying program benefits to eligible people. In many cases, particularly when evaluating a continuing program such as WIC, the denial of benefits to eligible applicants is not feasible.

As a result, many, if not most, evaluations of government programs are based on statistical comparisons of self-selected (as opposed to randomly assigned) groups of program participants and eligible nonparticipants. Such designs almost always have the potential of selection bias, which occurs when underlying and unobservable differences between program participants and a comparison group of nonparticipants create differences in outcomes that are incorrectly attributed to program participation. For example, if prenatal WIC participants are more motivated and concerned about health and nutrition than nonparticipants, birth outcomes of WIC participants may be better than those of nonparticipants even in the absence of the WIC program. Alternatively, if WIC is successful at targeting and enrolling women at the highest risk, any differences in birth outcomes between WIC participants and nonparticipants are likely to be understated as a result of preexisting differences in risk.

Clearly, selection bias is an important methodological limitation to evaluations of the WIC program. Therefore, what do we do about selection bias? Do we downplay all WIC evaluation findings based on quasi-experimental designs? Or do we conduct a careful and thorough analysis of both the potential of selection bias and its implications for estimated program effects? Although Besharov and Germanis are careful to detail the potential of selection bias, they never fully interpret how the evidence of selection bias in each of the studies may affect what we know about WIC's effectiveness. In essence, they downplay the findings of all evaluations because of the *potential* of selection bias. But several of the studies cited actually suggest that the potential for selection bias *understates* the results of WIC effects.

Consider the National WIC Evaluation, which found improved dietary and health outcomes for WIC infants and children relative to a comparison group of nonparticipating infants and children. As Peter H. Rossi discussed in his book *Feeding the Poor,* the comparison group was "markedly higher on most measures of socioeconomic status when compared with WIC participants."[1] The researchers from the National WIC Evaluation concluded that "because control women were clearly more privileged and affluent . . . the effect on the results is therefore in a specified direction: It is likely that the effects of WIC will tend to be obscured by the differences in prior characteristics of the study groups."[2] In other words, any estimated effects of the WIC program from the National WIC Evaluation are likely to be understated. Besharov and Germanis label those results as only "suggestive," but the research clearly shows that they are more than suggestive. In fact, the research strongly implies that the findings of improved dietary outcomes and health status of WIC participants would be even stronger with a more suitable comparison group.

Besharov and Germanis also criticize WIC studies of pregnant women and newborns for their failure to correct for selection bias. There, the criticism appears more justified, because several studies that attempted to deal with selection bias concluded that estimated program effects declined after the correction for selection bias. But what is missing from their analysis is a description of the technical difficulties in handling potential selection bias in the case of prenatal WIC participation. In particular, the models used to correct for selection issues are notoriously unstable. Numerous analyses of prenatal WIC participation that attempt to model and correct for selection bias find that the results are not consistent in sign and depend critically on the assumptions and estimation procedures used. For example, Besharov and Germanis cite an analysis by Anne Gordon and Lyle Nelson that examined the effects of prenatal WIC participation on birth outcomes. In their correction for selection bias, program effects either increased or decreased, in both cases by a large amount, depending on model specification and estimation procedures.

Even when the WIC studies do control successfully for the potential for selection bias, Besharov and Germanis question the findings. A study of dietary outcomes based on data from the 1989–1991 Continuing Survey of Food Intake by Individuals found increased intakes by WIC children for ten of fifteen nutrients examined, most notably iron and zinc.[3] Conducted by Donald Rose and others, that analysis was careful to consider the preexisting differences between the WIC children and other eligible non-WIC children, and it produced analysis results that controlled for those differences. Nevertheless, Besharov and Germanis criticize those findings because of the generic weaknesses of comparison groups.

In short, Besharov and Germanis seem to consider all WIC research flawed by selection bias. Even the studies that apparently control successfully for selection bias are suspect in their view, because of the weaknesses of quasi-experimental comparison group designs. If that criterion were to be applied more generally, we would have to conclude that program evaluation can be conducted only with randomized designs. Although clearly superior, randomized designs often are not practical, primarily because of ethical concerns associated with withholding program benefits from eligible people. If, as a result, we had chosen not to conduct any program evaluation because of the generic weaknesses of comparison group designs, as detailed by Besharov and Germanis, we would certainly know far less about the effects of WIC than we currently do.

In conclusion, selection bias is an important methodological limitation to the current research on WIC's effectiveness. Rather than dismiss the findings of all WIC program evaluations, a more productive approach would be to consider the sum of the evidence on WIC in light of the potential for selection bias. At a risk of oversimplifying, two thoughts may help clarify the findings from the existing WIC program evaluations that have been criticized for their treatment of the selection bias issue.

First, WIC improves birth outcomes, although it is possible that the estimated program effects may overstate true program effects because of both selection bias and gestational age bias. But a vast number of studies—conducted over different time periods, with different samples, and with many attempts to address those methodological issues—supports the conclusion that WIC improves birth outcomes.[4]

Second, WIC participation is associated with increased intake of the nutrients the program targets—iron, vitamin A, vitamin C, protein, and calcium—and a decrease in the proportion of people with very low nutrient intakes. Those findings do not change significantly when corrections for selection bias are estimated. As I discuss below, evidence also suggests an impact of WIC on iron-deficiency anemia.

What Do We Know about How WIC Affects Infants and Children?

Besharov and Germanis are particularly critical of the WIC research concerning the effects for infants and children. They are correct in noting that much less is known about WIC's effects on children. But to say that much less is known is not the same as saying that nothing is known about WIC's effects on that group.

If we start with the early WIC evaluations, especially the National WIC Evaluation, and continue with more recent studies of dietary intake, we find strong evidence that children's participation in the program improves nutrient intake.[5] Peter Rossi's analysis, which informed much of the Besharov and Germanis discussion, concluded that "fairly firm evidence of the positive effects of WIC on the nutrient intake of children aged one to four" exists. Besharov and Germanis question those findings of improved diets; they claim that the diets of most WIC children already exceed the recommended dietary allowances for many nutrients. That statement reflects a serious misunderstanding of how to interpret and use the recommended dietary allowances. The main problem is that one cannot use mean nutrient intake to make statements about nutrient adequacy; if one uses mean intakes in that way, they almost always are incorrect. For example, if mean intake of a subgroup equals the recommended dietary allowance for a specific nutrient, a very high proportion of people in that subgroup is likely to have an inadequate intake of that nutrient.[6]

More important, Besharov and Germanis question one of the most dramatic findings associated with the WIC program: the reduction in iron-deficiency anemia. Iron-deficiency anemia has long been one of the primary public health problems facing infants and children in the United States, especially low-income infants and children. Iron-deficiency anemia not only is a severe health problem but also leads to long-term deficits in cognitive development in children.

Over the period in which the WIC program has expanded, the prevalence of iron-deficiency anemia among low-income children has declined significantly. Besharov and Germanis are correct in questioning whether the entire decline can be attributed to the WIC program.

But a comparison of hematological tests of low-income children at enrollment in public health programs (primarily WIC) with tests at follow-up visits indicates declines in the prevalence of iron-deficiency anemia, a result that suggests positive effects of participation in the public health programs, especially the WIC program. In their review of the studies by Ray Yip and his colleagues, Besharov and Germanis state that the decline in iron-deficiency anemia could be explained by a change over time in the composition of the WIC caseload. Besharov and Germanis fail to note, however, that the Yip study specifically addressed that issue and found that it was unlikely that the trends observed could be a result of changes in the socioeconomic status of the WIC caseload.[7]

Besharov and Germanis also question the role of infant formula rebates, which have saved the WIC program millions of dollars over the years and allowed the program to expand. While their criticism seems to focus more on the expansion of the program, it also casts doubt on the rebate program. It is hard to see how one can argue with a program policy that produces considerable cost savings.

Besharov and Germanis note that information on the long-term effects of WIC participation on physical and cognitive development of children is limited. While true, that lack of information should not negate the research showing the effects of WIC on reducing iron-deficiency anemia and increasing nutrient intakes. A large body of literature already exists documenting the long-term behavioral and cognitive benefits from reducing iron-deficiency anemia and the health benefits of improved diets. Although further research on WIC's effects in those areas would be useful and important, existing research on the positive effects of WIC on such key mediating factors as iron-deficiency anemia and intake of nutrients is valid and useful in and of itself.

Where Do We Go from Here?

Despite problems with their review of the WIC research, Besharov and Germanis are correct in noting that many interesting policy options exist for improving the WIC program and learning more about its effects. In particular, they call for WIC to focus on addressing a major public health nutrition issue—the increasing prevalence of overweight children and adults. They argue forcefully that WIC is an ideal venue for understanding and addressing the issues related to poor diet choices and lack of physical activity.

Two of the six policy options introduced by Besharov and Germanis deserve special attention: targeting WIC resources to the most needy and testing alternative service configurations. The following discussion is not intended to discourage such policy options but to ensure that policymakers consider important issues when thinking about program experimentation.

Targeting. Besharov and Germanis propose targeting limited program resources to those at highest risk of poor nutrition and health outcomes. Although few people would argue with targeting limited program resources to those most in need, the need to target raises an interesting policy issue and tradeoff. The WIC priority system is supposed to target program resources to those at highest nutrition risk, yet the legislative objective of the WIC program is to prevent the occurrence of adverse nutrition and health risks. If WIC program benefits are targeted only to those already at risk, then the legislative objective of WIC cannot be satisfied.

More fundamentally, an important question facing policymakers is, If we think that the WIC program prevents nutrition and health problems, are we willing to target resources away from people who are not currently at high risk and take a chance that adverse outcomes may result? For example, Besharov and Germanis question the high percentage of infant formula purchased by WIC funds and suggest that WIC benefits are provided too broadly. Given the strong secular decline in iron-deficiency anemia associated with expansions in the WIC program for infants and children, it is hard to gamble with the health of infants and children by targeting benefits only to infants who already are iron-deficient or by eliminating infant formula rebates that have been responsible for increases in the WIC caseload.

Test Alternative Service Configurations. Besharov and Germanis propose integrating WIC into Medicaid managed care systems, presumably to eliminate parallel funding streams and to coordinate the services available to low-income women. Although that is an attractive idea in some respects, even Besharov and Germanis recognize the lack of attention many managed care organizations give to prevention—the underlying objective of the WIC program. In addition, although WIC has a strong referral component, WIC is a nutrition program, not a health program. The cornerstone of the WIC program is its provision of supplemental foods containing nutrients known to be lacking in the diets of low-income women, infants, and children. Any experimentation, such as that suggested by Besharov and Germanis, must recognize the nutrition underpinnings of the WIC program. Policy alternatives such as integrating the program into Medicaid managed care or relaxing WIC spending rules run the very real risk that the program benefits will be diluted and the nutrition foundation of the WIC program will be weakened.

Summary

In summary, Besharov and Germanis are correct in noting that studies of WIC effects have limitations and that the findings need to be interpreted carefully when considering policy changes that might improve the WIC program. But their attempt to provide a "frank treatment" of the WIC program involves a level of exaggeration equal to that of the studies they criticize. WIC may not have a three-to-one benefit-cost ratio for all sub-groups of participants, but the evidence is strong that some important nutrition and health benefits are associated with WIC participation: improved birth outcomes, reduced rates of iron-deficiency anemia, and improved diets. On the basis of an honest assessment of the WIC research, let us collectively pursue some of the interesting policy options proposed by Besharov and Germanis with the goal of strengthening and improving the WIC program.

13

Enhancing WIC's Effectiveness

Robert Greenstein

I appreciate the invitation of Douglas J. Besharov and Peter Germanis to comment on part 1 of this volume, "Rethinking WIC." They clearly have devoted considerable time to that study and offer a number of policy and research proposals, some of which merit consideration.

A good part of their analysis consists of a discussion of WIC research and other aspects of WIC that is largely at odds with reviews of the research literature on WIC conducted by various researchers and evaluators. Besharov and Germanis present a significantly less positive reading of the research than reviews of the research literature by the General Accounting Office, the Urban Institute, and Barbara L. Devaney of Mathematica Policy Research, who is perhaps the leading expert in the field. Unfortunately, their presentation of that research is not always balanced.

Their discussion of various other WIC program issues, such as use of the WIC nutritional risk criteria or changes over time in the incomes of WIC participants, is also problematic in some respects. Some of their assertions in those areas are unsupported or are based on data or results from studies that either have significant methodological weaknesses or are contradicted by other studies. The problems with Besharov and Germanis's discussion of WIC fall into three broad areas.

First, they do not accurately describe how policymakers have understood the research findings on WIC or how "advocates" have presented those findings. They set up a bit of a "straw man" with their suggestion that WIC policymaking has been conducted in an atmosphere in which it was widely and mistakenly believed that the research had found that each dollar expended in the *entire* WIC program generated three dollars in savings. Policymakers generally have not labored under such an illusion. Moreover, contrary to the contentions of "Rethinking WIC" that weaknesses in WIC research have been hidden from view, the policymaking community has widely discussed and well understood key weaknesses in past research—such as the weaknesses of the National WIC Evaluation of the 1980s.

Second, Besharov and Germanis present a reading of the research findings that underplays too greatly the research findings on WIC's effects in reducing low birthweight and anemia and improving children's diets, a point Barbara L. Devaney also makes in her comments.

Finally, "Rethinking WIC" contains various statements about the WIC program that are not adequately supported. Some of those statements are of questionable accuracy.

The policy recommendations section of "Rethinking WIC" has both strengths and weaknesses. Some of its proposals merit serious consideration, such as its call to give more emphasis in WIC to preventing obesity. Other recommendations, in my view, would be likely to reduce WIC's effectiveness, such as proposals to allow states to add food items to the WIC food package, an approach that risks leading to the addition of certain foods in some states because producers or processors of those foods are located in and have particular political clout in those states. In this chapter I discuss the principal areas of concern with the Besharov and Germanis study in turn and then evaluate some of the study's recommendations.

What Have Policymakers Understood and Program Proponents Said?

The Besharov and Germanis study suggests that WIC policymaking has been conducted in an atmosphere in which policymakers have mistakenly thought that each dollar invested in WIC produces three dollars in savings. In a recent article, Besharov and Germanis called that "the most common claim" about WIC.[1] In part 1, "Rethinking WIC," they state that "inflated benefit-cost estimates . . . have become part of the political landscape" and are cited by many advocates and politicians.

Assertions that many policymakers and advocates have falsely claimed that the three-to-one savings ratio applies to WIC as a whole are not accurate, however. In response to an earlier draft of Besharov and Germanis's study, staff at the Center on Budget and Policy Priorities examined all authorization and appropriations debates regarding WIC for a good part of the 1990s. We did not find a single instance in which a committee report, conference report, or statement by either the chairman or the ranking member of a committee or subcommittee with either authorization or appropriation jurisdiction over WIC misapplied that savings ratio.[2] Nor am I aware of any document by any advocacy group that incorrectly applies the three-to-one ratio to WIC as a whole rather than to the prenatal component of the program.

Besharov and Germanis cite a speech by former U.S. Department of Agriculture Undersecretary Shirley Watkins and an op-ed by former Health and Human Services Secretary Louis Sullivan that are incorrect in that regard. The Sullivan op-ed ran in 1995, long after Sullivan ceased being a policymaker. The Watkins speech was likely written by a USDA speechwriter and not sent for review to the appropriate officials in the Food and Nutrition Service, the USDA agency that oversees WIC. As far back as the late 1970s, the Food and Nutrition Service informed the USDA secretary's office that the three-to-one ratio, cited in studies in that period, applied to the prenatal component of WIC and not to WIC as a whole.[3]

Throughout the period of WIC expansion, the key decisionmakers in the USDA, the Office of Management and Budget, and the relevant congressional committees have understood that matter correctly. In 1993 OMB's associate director for human resources even convened a lengthy briefing with leading outside researchers to review what the research does and does not show about WIC. That Undersecretary Watkins gave one speech that misstated those findings is not of much significance here. The WIC program had already reached its current size before she assumed her post. WIC reached the 7.4 million participation level in the summer of 1996 and has not grown since; Watkins assumed her post in 1997. Moreover, the WIC research findings that policymakers and WIC proponents have cited in recent years are largely the findings of the GAO and are based on its comprehensive evaluation of studies of WIC, a subsequent review of the WIC research literature by the Urban Institute (which is not discussed in the Besharov-Germanis study),[4] and several research papers by Devaney.

In the same vein, Besharov and Germanis write that it has been "politically incorrect to acknowledge the limitations of past research." At best, that is a substantial exaggeration. For example, some of the most positive research findings on WIC are those of the National WIC Evaluation. For years, those findings have not figured in a major way in WIC policy discussions because of that evaluation's methodological weaknesses, which analysts widely noted.

The Research Findings

Besharov and Germanis contend that "beyond modest reductions in anemia and modest increases in the intake of selected nutrients, little research evidence exists about the effectiveness" of WIC, except for its prenatal component. They contend that even WIC's effects in reducing the incidence of low birthweight are "modest at best." Where positive research findings exist on WIC, Besharov and Germanis downplay the findings and generally term them "small" or "modest." To some extent, their study damns WIC with faint praise. A number of other researchers and evaluators have looked at the same body of research as Besharov and Germanis and have come to different conclusions.

WIC's Effects on Birth Outcomes. Besharov and Germanis challenge the GAO evaluation that examined WIC's effects on birth outcomes. Some background on the GAO report is in order.

In the early 1990s, several members of Congress asked the GAO to determine how much was saved as a result of each dollar spent in an array of social programs for children. To the chagrin of the members who requested the study, the GAO reported back that in every program but one, the research was inadequate to establish a benefit-cost ratio. The GAO's conclusions were hardly what children's advocates were seeking.

The sole place in which such a ratio could be established, the GAO said, was in the prenatal component of WIC. The GAO reviewed all research on WIC's effects on low birthweight. It discarded a large number of studies that it concluded were affected too greatly by selection bias or other methodological problems. The GAO concluded, however, that a number of the studies were sufficiently strong and that conclusions could be drawn from them. On the basis of its review, the GAO estimated that the prenatal component of WIC reduced the incidence of low birthweight by 25 percent, reduced the incidence of very low birthweight by 44 percent, and produced savings of $3.50 for each dollar invested in the prenatal component of WIC. Such results are not small or modest.

Besharov and Germanis disagree with the GAO report. They cite methodological weaknesses in the studies the GAO used. The points they raise concerning those studies are not new; the GAO evaluators were well aware of those issues and considered them in determining which studies to discard and which met their standards. The GAO concluded that a number of those studies, while not perfect, were strong.

Besharov and Germanis essentially argue that the GAO and other reviewers who have concluded that the research indicates that WIC has strong effects in reducing low birthweight are mistaken. A proper reading of that research, they contend, suggests that WIC has no or only a small effect in reducing low birthweight. Besharov and Germanis's approach to that research question leads to an understatement of what the research shows.

For example, they state that if one controls for differences in "gestational age"—the number of weeks at which an infant is born—a substantial part of WIC's reported effects in reducing the incidence of low birthweight disappears. As Devaney and other researchers have pointed out, however, controlling for gestational age distorts and understates WIC's effects. The research literature shows that WIC increases gestational age—it leads to longer pregnancies, on average—and that this is a key mechanism through which WIC increases birthweights. Controlling for gestational age thus "controls away" a significant portion of WIC's effects in raising birthweights.

Besharov and Germanis acknowledge that controlling for gestational age may understate WIC's effects but argue that controls are needed to prevent the presence of women who entered WIC late in their pregnancies from biasing the research results. That is a valid point. One can deal with that concern, however, by excluding late-entrant pregnant women from research analyses. Work by Devaney and others suggests that when that step is taken, the findings of WIC's effect in reducing low birthweight remain rather robust.

In another part of their discussion of the effects of WIC on birthweight, Besharov and Germanis report that one study found that providing WIC to postpartum women increased the average birthweight of the next children those women bore by 4 percent, an improvement they term "small." That 4 percent improvement translates, however, into an average gain in birthweight of 131 grams, an impressive result. Whether particular results are "small" may be in the eye of the beholder, but many researchers and medical professionals would find various improvements that Besharov and Germanis term "small" or "modest" to be quite significant from the standpoint of public health. Besharov and Germanis raise other issues about the study of postpartum women that I shall not address here. My point here is not to debate the merits of that particular study but to raise concerns about the use of terms such as *small* and *modest* in certain places in the study.

WIC's Effects on Children. Besharov and Germanis downplay the significance of research conducted at the Centers for Disease Control on WIC's effects in reducing child anemia. They argue that CDC researchers' findings of a sharp decrease in anemia among children in the WIC program could simply be part of a broader downward trend in child anemia in the country caused by factors other than WIC or that it could be a result of a change over a number of years in the composition of the children enrolled in WIC.

The work of the CDC researchers does indicate that a portion of the decrease in child anemia stems from a general improvement in the iron nutritional status of U.S. children. The CDC research also indicates, however, that the WIC program has made an important contribution to reducing anemia. Specifically, the CDC researchers compared the anemia levels of infants and children at the time of initial enrollment in WIC with the anemia levels of infants and children at WIC follow-up visits. They found reductions in anemia rates for most age groups of infants and young children in most years for which they examined data. The researchers reported that "the prevalence of anemia . . . was consistently higher for those children seen at initial visits compared with those seen at follow-up visits."[5] Devaney and other health and medical researchers have observed that the CDC research indicates that WIC has important effects in reducing anemia. Changes over a number of years in child anemia trends nationally and changes over time in the WIC caseload cannot account for the differences in anemia rates between children at the time of enrollment in WIC and children at the time of WIC follow-up visits.[6]

Besharov and Germanis also seek to downplay the findings of WIC's effects in lowering anemia by stating that "if there had been a socially significant reduction in anemia, one would expect, for example, to see it reflected in a reduction in the behaviors associated with anemia." The implication is that because we lack evidence of a reduction in those behaviors, WIC may not produce a significant effect in reducing anemia.

We lack strong evidence of a distinct link between WIC and a reduction in anemia-related behaviors, however, because that link has not been much studied. That does not mean that such a link may not exist. Indeed, some evidence of such a link exists; the National WIC Evaluation found evidence of an association between WIC and improved cognitive functioning in children. That finding must be treated with caution because of the methodological problems of the evaluation, but as Devaney points out in her comments on part 1, "Rethinking WIC," the selection-bias problems affecting the National WIC Evaluation made that study more likely to *understate* WIC's effects than to overstate them.

The bottom line is that significant evidence indicates that WIC re-duces child anemia, and anemia has been shown to have significant health consequences for children. Anemia is associated with adverse effects on cognitive and behavioral developments. Moreover, the reduction in ane-mia is plausible, given evidence that WIC leads to higher dietary iron intakes, as discussed below. Iron deficiency is the leading cause of ane-mia in children.

Besharov and Germanis's treatment of the research on WIC's effects on children's diets appears to have a similar coloration. A 1998 study by Donald Rose, Jean-Pierre Habicht, and Barbara L. Devaney on the ef-fects of WIC on the diets of preschool children found WIC to have sig-nificant effects in increasing children's intakes of ten nutrients.[7] Three of the nutrients—iron, zinc, and vitamin E—are among the four nutri-ents most frequently deficient in the diets of preschool children. Par-ticularly impressive are the study's findings that WIC substantially increases the intakes of iron and zinc, crucial nutrients for health.

Besharov and Germanis downplay the significance of that study, too, by raising methodological concerns. Methodological concerns can be raised about any study that does not use "random assignment," but top-notch researchers meticulously conducted the study, and it is generally considered quite solid. Despite the impressive findings of that study, Besharov and Germanis pronounce that "in all, WIC probably makes little significant difference in the diets of one- to four-year-old children," although they acknowledge that important effects could exist for some groups of children. That is not the conclusion to which the study leads or the conclusion that most researchers with experience in studying children's diets would draw.

The findings of the National WIC Evaluation, which found large ef-fects of WIC on improving children's diets, are also of note in that re-gard. Besharov and Germanis dismiss those findings because of the selection-bias problems in that evaluation. As Devaney has explained, however, the WIC children in that study were more disadvantaged than the non-WIC children with whom they were compared. As a result, as noted above, the selection-bias problems that affected the study would likely cause it to understate WIC's positive effects on children's diets rather than to overstate them.

The various findings on WIC's effects on children can be looked at together. Studies indicate that WIC both substantially improves the in-takes of iron and other nutrients among children and reduces iron-deficiency anemia among children. Those results, from different studies, reinforce each other. They indicate that WIC has significant positive effects on children. The findings regarding WIC's effects on children are, in fact, stronger than those for many other highly regarded children's programs, such as the school lunch program.

WIC and Healthy Start. One interesting part of Besharov and Germanis's discussion of the research is their attempt to apply research findings on the Healthy Start program to WIC. They imply that research indicating that Healthy Start has been ineffective suggests that WIC is likely to be less effective than commonly thought, because WIC has much in common with Healthy Start. They base their discussion on an interim study that found few positive effects of Healthy Start. But the final evaluation report on Healthy Start concludes that Healthy Start was, in fact, associated with better outcomes for children in some—but not all—communities, such as improved prenatal care utilization (eight of fifteen project areas), reductions in premature births (four of fifteen project areas), reductions in low-birthweight rates (three of fifteen project areas for low birthweight and three of fifteen project areas for very low birthweight), and reductions in infant mortality (two of fifteen project areas).[8] (Healthy Start emphasized local flexibility, and programs differed substantially from community to community.)

Also problematic is Besharov and Germanis's statement that "Healthy Start spends an average of $146 per month for each maternal participant—more than three times as much as WIC. Hence, one would have expected it to do at least as well as WIC—if the WIC findings are valid." That statement is unwarranted, because WIC and Healthy Start are quite different. Healthy Start provides no food package and is purely a services program, an important point because some research suggests that it is the WIC food package that may be primarily responsible for WIC's effects in improving birthweight. In short, in citing the lack of evidence for Healthy Start's efficacy from a preliminary study of Healthy Start as an indication that WIC must not have strong effects either, the authors display a tendency to draw selectively from the research literature in a way that supports their conclusions.

A researcher with a longer history and deeper body of work on medical evaluation than Besharov and Germanis—Leighton Ku, then with the Urban Institute—read the same research as the authors and came to different conclusions. In an article in the *Public Interest*, Ku wrote, "While the research evidence about WIC's effectiveness is not perfect, it is hard to think of any public program with so consistent a body of positive research findings."[9]

Is WIC Cost-Effective? Besharov and Germanis contend that a proper reading of the research yields the conclusion that WIC is probably not cost-effective and "would likely fail a benefit-cost test." Besharov and Germanis's assertion may create misimpressions among readers, who may think that the authors are saying that WIC is an ineffective program.

The basis for their assertion is that no research quantifies what savings in health care and other costs may result from each dollar spent on the nonprenatal component of WIC. Given WIC's effects in reducing anemia, some such savings are likely. But those savings are extremely difficult to identify and almost impossible to quantify.

Given their negative reading of the research, Besharov and Germanis conclude that each dollar spent on WIC as a whole probably does not save one dollar in other costs. But no study has been conducted on that matter; their judgment on the issue is purely speculative. Moreover, even if such a conclusion proved to be true, it would hardly mean that WIC is an ineffective program. WIC's impact in reducing low birthweight and anemia and improving diets (not to mention its apparent success in causing more children to receive immunizations and other health care) would make it an effective program even if it turned out that the program as a whole generated less than one dollar in savings for each dollar expended. Few programs exist anywhere in the federal government (and few tax incentives either, for that matter) for which we have evidence that each dollar spent generates more than one dollar in savings. Producing hard savings elsewhere in the budget is not the basic test of whether a social program has been effective in fulfilling its mission.

Other Claims about the WIC Program

The Besharov-Germanis study makes various assertions about WIC that are questionable or overstated. For example, the study portrays WIC as a program in which participation continues to grow. "More expansions of WIC are looming," it declares. In fact, participation reached 7.4 million in the summer of 1996 and essentially has been flat since then or has declined slightly.[10]

In another unsupported assertion, they state that "most agencies seem to have assumed that *all* income-eligible applicants are at nutritional risk." In a footnote, the authors acknowledge that "little systematic evidence . . . exists" for that claim. Moreover, the study notes elsewhere that the number of four-year-olds in the program is much smaller than the number of younger children. One reason could be that fewer four-year-old children meet the nutritional risk test.

The manner in which the program's nutritional risk criteria are applied appears to vary across states. A blanket statement that most agencies ignore those criteria is, however, unwarranted. An alternative explanation could be that, in fact, the overwhelming bulk of those who meet the WIC income criteria also meet the program's nutritional risk tests. Indeed, the USDA recently released a study by Sigma One that provides new estimates of the proportion of WIC income-eligibles who are at nutritional risk. Those new estimates are based on more recent data from the National Maternal and Infant Health Survey and the National Health and Nutrition Examination Survey (NHANES III, 1988–1994).[11] The recent study estimates that about 90 percent of income-eligible infants and children and about 95 percent of the income-eligible pregnant women are at nutritional risk. Those percentages are somewhat higher than the ones used in the past, which were based on older survey data. In short, the contention that most WIC agencies are ignoring the nutritional risk criteria is not supported by research. It is also plausible that some WIC agencies may apply the nutritional risk criteria more rigorously to older children than to pregnant women and infants because of concerns that denying WIC to low-income pregnant women and infants who do not yet quite meet the nutritional risk criteria could undermine WIC's preventive role and result in some of those women and infants' developing significant problems at a critical stage of growth and development.

Another questionable assertion is the study's contention that WIC infant formula cost containment

> has provided billions of dollars to WIC with little legislative oversight. . . . Coming to the program outside the normal appropriations process, those billions of dollars have been automatically applied under WIC's eligibility and funding rules—without considering whether the additional funds should be used to adjust program benefits or services.

That assertion is incorrect. Virtually every WIC reauthorization debate of the past twelve years has been marked by congressional consideration of the uses to which WIC rebate savings should be put and of the extent to which those savings should go to administrative costs and services, as distinguished from WIC food benefits. The current rules the program follows in that regard did not escape congressional oversight; to the contrary, they are the result of the laws Congress has passed.

It is also not accurate to characterize infant formula rebate savings as currently being used to expand WIC participation; as noted, participation has not risen since mid-1996. With participation flat or fluctuating in a small range, the principal use of those savings is to reduce the costs the federal government otherwise would incur in maintaining WIC participation.[12] It is also curious that Besharov and Germanis say little about the extraordinary success of WIC infant formula cost containment, under which many states secure savings equal to 80 or 90 percent of the wholesale price of the formula, in improving program efficiency. WIC infant formula cost containment may be the most successful cost containment system in any health-related program at any level of government.

The study's treatment of issues related to WIC participation and eligibility is also flawed. Besharov and Germanis state that the proportion of WIC participants in the higher parts of the WIC income eligibility scale has grown substantially over the past decade and that 29 percent of WIC participants have incomes over $25,000. Those statements are contradicted, however, by the studies that the USDA issues approximately every two years on the characteristics of WIC participants.

The WIC characteristics studies show almost no change in the proportion of higher-income participants in the programs through 1996. Those studies, based on a census of administrative data for virtually all WIC participants, found that throughout that period, about three-quarters of participants (73 to 77 percent of those for whom data were present) had incomes at or below the poverty line and very few (6 to 7 percent) had incomes above 150 percent of the poverty line. The WIC participant characteristics study for 1998 found a small reduction in the proportion of participants with incomes at or below the poverty line (to 69 percent) and a slight increase in the share with incomes greater than 150 percent of poverty (to 9 percent).[13] It is not clear whether that represents a small change or is a statistical aberration caused by an increase in the level of missing data in the 1998 survey. It is possible, given the strong economic growth and reduction in poverty that occurred in the late 1990s, that WIC participants' income grew slightly in the last part of the 1990s, but there does not appear to have been a broad pattern of change over the past two decades as the WIC caseload increased. Regardless of whether that small change in the income distribution of WIC participants is valid, the WIC administrative data show that in all years the large majority of WIC participants had incomes below the poverty line and relatively few had higher incomes.

The income figures that Besharov and Germanis cite come from an unpublished analysis by Richard Bavier that uses data from the Survey of Income and Program Participation. The figures are problematic for several reasons. The survey data have an important weakness—they miss large numbers of WIC participants. An analysis that Mathematica Policy Research published in 1997 found that the survey data that Mathematica examined missed 24 percent of all infants and children in WIC, including 43 percent of the infants. By contrast, the data from the WIC characteristics studies do not suffer from that problem. They are drawn not from a sample, as the Survey of Income and Program Participation is, but from a census of nearly all WIC participant files in the nation in April of every even-numbered year. The 1996 study is based on about 8 million WIC records. The survey data, by contrast, are based on samples that included several hundred or several thousand WIC participants.

Moreover, Besharov and Germanis acknowledge that Bavier cautioned that methodological problems compromise his analysis, but they use the Bavier findings anyway. They state, "Nevertheless, his findings are consistent with informal reports from the field [none of which are cited] and common sense." They do not mention that his findings are inconsistent with the WIC characteristics surveys. They also somewhat inflate the Bavier findings at one point in their study, when they state that "one-third" of WIC participants have incomes over $25,000; Bavier's figures place that number at 29 percent. Their handling of those data is troubling. It suggests that the authors may be more concerned with potential methodological weaknesses in studies that do not support their conclusions than with weaknesses in studies that lend them support.

To be sure, the data in the WIC characteristics surveys are not perfect. They reflect income at the time that people apply or are recertified for WIC; the income of some families may rise during their WIC certification periods. But the consistent pattern over many years in the characteristics surveys raises serious doubts about Besharov and Germanis's claims of substantially rising income levels among WIC participants.

Besharov and Germanis are convinced that the income profile of WIC participants must have risen substantially over time because WIC participation has expanded. They think that common sense indicates that this must have occurred. But that is not necessarily so. When states have insufficient WIC funds to serve all eligible applicants, they are required to institute a priority system. The priority system is based *not* on the applicant's income but on the applicant's health and nutritional risk status and on whether the applicant is a pregnant woman, breastfeeding woman, postpartum woman, infant, or child. Women and infants generally rank higher on the priority scale than children. Not surprisingly, as WIC participation grew during the 1990s, a disproportionate share of the participation growth occurred among children.[14]

The authors' treatment of data on the percentage of people eligible for WIC who participate in the program also warrants mention. Besharov and Germanis cite estimates from the U.S. Department of Agriculture that seem to indicate that the number of infants and breast-feeding or postpartum women participating in WIC exceeds the number who are eligible. Recognition is widespread, however, that those estimates are seriously flawed and are likely to lead to a substantial undercount of the eligible population. Because the number of people who are eligible for WIC is understated in those estimates, a misimpression can be created that some categories of enrollees participate at rates well in excess of 100 percent. Indeed, the USDA—which itself believes that those estimates are problematic—recently asked the National Academy of Sciences to provide more rigorous estimates of the number of people eligible for WIC. The NAS has convened an expert panel to conduct that work. To lay out the technical issues related to estimating the number of eligible people, Mathematica Policy Research recently issued a major study, which identifies an array of problems with the USDA estimates. The material in the Mathematica study indicates that the estimates that Besharov and Germanis cite and rely upon are likely to understate substantially the number of people who are eligible for WIC.[15]

For reasons such as those, the USDA's Economic Research Service informed congressional staff in 1999 that the estimates the USDA has been using of the number of people eligible for WIC are likely to be excessively low. If the number of people eligible for WIC is significantly higher than those USDA estimates assumed, as is likely to be the case, then actual WIC participation rates are lower than the participation-rate estimates that Besharov and Germanis cite.

Policy Recommendations

In part 1 of this volume, Besharov and Germanis provide some useful policy recommendations—particularly their call for consideration of how WIC might help reduce obesity. In that regard, it should be noted that the USDA, the CDC, and five WIC state agencies initiated a series of projects in September 1999 aimed at improving WIC's role as an intervention to prevent child obesity.

A number of the study's policy recommendations are motivated, however, by a view that policymakers should reduce the number of WIC participants and provide larger WIC food packages for some participants and increased WIC-funded services for other participants. Although some proposals for enriched services may be worth considering, I think that such an approach is unwise.

Besharov and Germanis believe that the WIC income limits are excessively high. In most states the general income limit is 185 percent of the poverty line, currently $26,178 for a family of three and $31,543 for a family of four. But most states have set income limits for their child health insurance programs at similar levels. That is also the income cut-off for reduced-price school meals. Given that a key part of WIC's mission is preventive, it seems reasonable to set WIC eligibility at that level.[16]

Besharov and Germanis observe that nearly half the infants in the nation enroll in WIC, which they take as an indication that eligibility is excessively broad. But as Leighton Ku has pointed out, so many infants are enrolled because close to half the infants in the United States live in families with incomes below 185 percent of the poverty line at some point during infancy. Family incomes tend to fall during infancy because many mothers stop working or reduce their work hours during a child's first year of life.

Before the reauthorization of WIC in 1998, the GAO and some policymakers raised certain concerns regarding administration of the WIC eligibility criteria. In response, steps have been taken to tighten administration. The 1998 reauthorization legislation tightened income documentation and other requirements. In addition, the program's nutritional risk criteria were modified in 1999, in response to recommendations made by the Institute of Medicine and others.

I am particularly concerned about Besharov and Germanis's recommendation to allow states to receive waivers to add more food to the WIC food packages for some categories of participants. The WIC food packages are based on the best scientific judgment of the American Academy of Pediatrics and other medical experts about the nutrients and foods, and the quantities of such foods, that women, infants, and young children need in their diets. The food packages contain large quantities of infant formula, milk or cheese, orange juice, and other items. For most categories of WIC participants, it is difficult to imagine that participants could consume much more of those food items.

Besharov and Germanis probably envision not that food items already in the food packages would be increased but that states would be allowed to include additional food items. Such a course would be ill-advised; its likely outcome would be that state agricultural or food-processing lobbies would pressure their states to add foods grown or manufactured in the state to the WIC food packages. Federal WIC funds ought not to be used to add foods to the program in response to political pressures from particular segments of the food industry that are strong in a given state.

That is not an idle fear. Throughout WIC's history, senators and congressmen have lobbied the USDA aggressively to have home-state products added to the WIC food package. Administrations of both parties have resisted such encroachments. The story would likely be different at the state level in cases in which the relative power of a particular segment of the food industry is much greater than at the national level.[17]

Over the course of the WIC program's history, the federal government has responded to new medical research by periodically revising the WIC food package by adding new foods and cutting back on foods no longer thought to add as much nutritional value. Several years ago, for example, the USDA substantially expanded the food package for breastfeeding women. A new review of the WIC food packages is currently underway at the USDA to consider new findings from the third National Health and Nutrition Examination Survey and new recommendations on dietary requirements from the National Academy of Sciences. Future reviews will undoubtedly be conducted as additional scientific information develops.

That is the appropriate way to proceed. It is unlikely that many states would have the resources to conduct as thorough or rigorous a review of the medical research in that area as the USDA does. Nor do states have reason to duplicate the USDA's work in that area.

Besharov and Germanis promote their proposal for states to be able to add foods to the WIC food package as an approach that would enable the food packages to be larger for poorer WIC families. Calibrating food benefits to income, however, is what the food stamp program does. If poorer families are receiving a full WIC package designed to reflect the best medical evidence, it is not clear that WIC should also seek to perform a food stamp–like function of further boosting the food purchases of those families. Varying WIC food packages by income status could also add to administrative complexity and burdens.

Besharov and Germanis also recommend shifting dollars from WIC foods to services, but strong evidence does not exist to support such a course. In addition, care would need to be taken to avoid the diversion of federal funds from WIC foods to the funding of services that a state already may be offering and financing with state dollars. Shifting WIC funds from foods to services in such circumstances would result in supplantation of state funds, not intensification of services.

Enriched prenatal services can be an adjunct to nutritional supplementation but are not a substitute for it. That some women might need more prenatal counseling, case management, or better access to health and social services does not mean they need fewer supplemental foods.

On another issue, the study is correct in noting that questions exist about whether the funds the federal government provides to state WIC agencies for nutrition services and administration are sufficient to administer the program and deliver adequately the services WIC is charged with providing. Besharov and Germanis note that the number of services that WIC programs must provide has increased over time. At the same time, the grants for nutrition services and administration that states receive have been adjusted annually for inflation and increases in WIC participation since 1987. If economies of scale exist in the provision of nutrition services and administration, states should have benefited from them as WIC participation grew.

In any event, the 1998 WIC reauthorization legislation mandated a major study of that matter, which the GAO is conducting, so that policymakers may ascertain whether grants for nutrition services and administration are adequate. The study should provide useful information on such an important issue. Grants to states for nutrition services and administration may need to be increased.

Besharov and Germanis offer several other appealing proposals. Could home-visitor programs be expanded? Can school-based services of the type that WIC provides, such as nutrition counseling, be expanded?

A question here is whether WIC is the best vehicle to deliver such services. In the case of school-based services, I think not. WIC runs through health agencies and clinics and is not situated at schools. Requiring stretched, low-income, working parents of schoolchildren to come to WIC clinics to receive such services seems inefficient. Such services would probably be better delivered at the school through a school-based program, rather than through WIC. The case concerning home-visitor services is less clear. WIC experiments in that area may have value. It is not clear whether WIC would be the best vehicle through which to provide those services.

Finally, Besharov and Germanis suggest allowing WIC benefits to be terminated for failure by a participant to meet various behavioral requirements. Policymakers should approach that issue with considerable caution. Should WIC food packages be terminated for a nutritionally at-risk pregnant woman if she fails to comply with a requirement? Would that not increase the chances that her baby would be born at a low birthweight? Besharov and Germanis cite an apparently successful experiment that used WIC "sanctions" as part of an effort to prod more parents of WIC children to secure immunizations for their children. Those sanctions, however, involved requiring the parents to pick up their WIC vouchers every month, rather than every two months, until the children were immunized; the sanctions did not terminate their WIC benefits. The issues here differ in important respects from the application of behavioral requirements to welfare receipt, with an attendant cutoff of benefits.

In conclusion, Besharov and Germanis have set forth a series of interesting ideas for changes in WIC, some of which I think deserve consideration. I find some of their other ideas troubling and believe that they would be more likely to reduce, rather than to enhance, WIC's effectiveness.

Notes

Notes

PART ONE
Chapter 1: Introduction

1. See Glickman (1997).
2. See Sullivan (1995).
3. This report simply asserted the importance of diet: "Hunger and malnutrition constitute a national emergency which requires an immediacy of response fully commensurate with the scope and severity. Delays are intolerable either in initiating relief, or in developing and funding long-term programs for remedy and prevention." Quoted in Rush et al. ("Background," 1988, 389–90). See also Rossi (1998, 45).
4. *U.S. Code of Federal Regulations,* 7 CFR 246.1.
5. See Rossi (1998, 64–65).
6. See Martin et al. (1999).
7. See Rossi (1998, 110).
8. See Huntington and Connell (1994, 1306–7).

Chapter 2: Program Benefits

1. Some states use alternative food delivery systems, such as home delivery, a centralized distribution center (warehouse), and electronic benefit transfer.
2. Most states have implemented efforts to keep the cost of the WIC food package down, such as limiting participation to stores that offer competitive prices and requiring participants to purchase specific brands. See U.S. General Accounting Office (1997b).
3. The seven categories are infants from birth to three months; infants from four to twelve months; women and children with special dietary needs; children from one to five years old; pregnant and breastfeeding women (basic);

postpartum, nonbreastfeeding women; and breastfeeding women (enhanced). The amount and type of food within each category may vary, depending on the type of recipient and the specific nutritional need.

4. *U.S. Code of Federal Regulations,* 7 CFR 246.10(c)(3).

5. The substitution of food is permitted to accommodate different cultural eating patterns and the special needs of homeless people. But state WIC agencies must submit such a request to the U.S. Department of Agriculture for approval. A substitute food must be nutritionally equivalent or superior to the food it replaces, widely available to participants, and no more expensive than the food it replaces.

6. States are required to pursue such "cost-containment" strategies as obtaining rebates from infant formula manufacturers, a practice that saved $1.4 billion in 1999. Essentially, the rebate savings must be used to expand program participation, as described in this volume.

7. See Kramer-LeBlanc et al. (1999, ES-8).

8. The researchers found that infants and children were generally achieving the recommended nutrient intake levels. For children, however, there was a concern about low levels of zinc intake.

9. See Kramer-LeBlanc et al. (1999, ES-3).

10. See Rossi (1998, 112).

11. Ibid., 63.

12. See U.S. General Accounting Office (1999, 25).

13. The initial figure was established in 1987 on the basis of the average nationwide cost per participant.

14. See Macro International, Inc., and Urban Institute (1995). The purpose of the research was to "study the impact of participation growth associated with infant-formula rebates, new regulatory and legislative requirements, and economic factors that occurred since 1988." During the period of the study (1988 to 1993), WIC's caseload grew by 45 percent.

15. See Miller (1999, 9).

16. See Fox et al. (1999, xi).

17. Ibid., xii.

18. Ibid., 5–6.

19. See Rossi (1998, 55).

20. See Fox et al. (1999, 2–4).

21. Ibid., 3–13.

Chapter 3: Program Coverage

1. For the proportion of infants participating, see U.S. General Accounting Office (1998, 1). In 1997 3.8 million children participated in WIC. The U.S. Department of Agriculture estimates that this number constituted 75 percent of eligible children. (See table 3-2.) Thus, nearly 1.3 million children were eligible but not participating—nearly 10 percent of the 15 million children ages one to five.

2. States may set maximum income eligibility limits between 100 and 185 percent of poverty, but all use the maximum guidelines.

3. That provision was intended to simplify eligibility determination. Several states, however, have expanded Medicaid eligibility, primarily through waivers and the state Children's Health Insurance Program, beyond 185 percent of poverty, currently the maximum income limit specified for WIC. That expansion has effectively increased WIC eligibility in those states as well.

4. See U.S. Department of Agriculture, Food and Consumer Service (1997, 1–2). Some states use a fourth criterion, "predisposing risk conditions," such as homelessness and migrancy.

5. *U.S. Code of Federal Regulations*, 7 CFR 246.

6. See Institute of Medicine (1996, 7).

7. See Rossi (1998, 98).

8. See U.S. Department of Agriculture (1998).

9. The criteria were tightened in two ways. First, the cutoff points or thresholds are "based on prevailing scientific data," so states have less discretion to implement them "loosely." Second, the scientific review led the USDA to drop some criteria, because "they do not reflect conditions that can be effectively addressed through the WIC benefit package nor do they constitute nutritionally related conditions." Examples of the two dozen risk criteria dropped include maternal short stature, abnormal postpartum weight change, pregnancy at age older than thirty-five, and low level of maternal education or literacy. Nevertheless, some criteria, such as "inadequate diet," still appear to be fairly open-ended. See U.S. Department of Agriculture (1998).

10. See U.S. General Accounting Office (1999, 23).

11. In 1994 WIC's name, the Special Supplemental Food Program for Women, Infants, and Children, was changed to the Special Supplemental Nutrition Program for Women, Infants, and Children.

12. See U.S. Department of Agriculture, Food and Nutrition Service, Office of Analysis and Evaluation (1999a, 1).

13. In 1999 24 percent of WIC participants were women (about 12 percent were pregnant, 5 percent were breastfeeding, and 7 percent were postpartum). See U.S. Department of Agriculture, Food and Nutrition Service, Office of Analysis and Evaluation (2001, 1).

14. The 1999 spending level for each target group was estimated by adding the average monthly administrative cost of $12 to the average monthly cost of food in 1999 for each target group and then multiplying the total by the average monthly number of recipients in each target group. That monthly cost was multiplied by twelve to arrive at an annual cost. Data for those estimates are from U.S. Department of Agriculture, Food and Nutrition Service, Office of Analysis and Evaluation (2000a, 2).

15. See U.S. Department of Agriculture, Food and Nutrition Service, Office of Analysis and Evaluation (1999b). The nutritional risk estimates are based on health survey data and approximate the percentage of the income-eligible population who also have at least one nutritional risk. It is estimated

that infants are most likely to have a nutritional risk (95 percent) and older children are least likely to have one (75 percent).

16. Note that this is a percentage of the estimated eligible population. It is possible that not all eligible people are participating and that more "ineligibles" exist than the 122 percent participation rate suggests.

17. See Randall, Bartlett, and Kennedy (1998, 36).

18. See U.S. Department of Agriculture, Food and Nutrition Service, Office of Analysis and Evaluation (2000a, 2).

19. See Fox et al. (1999, xiv). The study reported, "This was the only program characteristic that was consistently included in the top three positive aspects of the WIC Program."

20. Like so many other areas of WIC implementation, little systematic evidence of such practices exists. But that is the most likely explanation for estimated participation levels that otherwise imply that all income-eligible people are at nutritional risk, even as medical evidence indicates otherwise. Compare Rossi (1998, 98) with Institute of Medicine (1996, 7).

21. See Lewis and Ellwood (1998).

22. As noted in table 3-2, the 69 percent participation estimate for pregnant women is artificially low, because it is unlikely that such women could participate a full forty weeks.

23. Personal communication from Richard Bavier to Peter Germanis, June 22, 1999, describing special tabulations by Richard Bavier of persons covered by WIC in the first six months of the 1988 panel of the Survey of Income and Program Participation and the first six months of the 1996 panel.

24. Those estimates are based on the assumption that the cost of each new participant equaled the average cost of serving any WIC participant. The amount of infant formula rebate savings is based on USDA information as reported in a stand-alone chart provided by the Center on Budget and Policy Priorities, "WIC Infant Formula Rebate Savings."

25. Tennessee has raised its income eligibility limit to 400 percent of poverty for families without access to employer coverage.

26. See Krause (1999).

Chapter 4: Previous Research

1. "Budget Mask," *Washington Post,* June 15, 1998, p. A22.

2. A number of studies often cited as part of literature documenting WIC's success are not included in this review but are summarized in Gordon and Nelson (1995). The studies suffer from the same methodological problems as the studies reviewed in this volume, and because they are older, they are less representative of the current WIC program than the newer studies.

3. See Ku (1999, 108).

4. See Caan et al. (1987).

5. The mean birthweight of infants born to mothers in the "extended" feeding group was 3,468 grams, 131 grams (3.8 percent) higher than the mean

birthweight of infants born to mothers in the "limited" feeding group. Although about 20 percent of the original study population was dropped because of missing information, the authors concluded that the bias that difference could introduce was limited. They estimated that the impact of WIC would be reduced by only about one-third, even when using extreme assumptions about the characteristics of the sample cases dropped.

6. See Rush et al. ("Longitudinal Study," 1988, 463). The researchers cautioned that those rates were unusually high and may have reflected a high nonresponse rate to the survey for women who chose not to breastfeed. In addition, they noted that it would have been useful to have information on the number who continued to breastfeed after hospital discharge and for how long they did so.

7. See Schwartz et al. (1992).

8. See Ku, Cohen, and Pindus (1994, 5).

9. See Rush et al. ("Study of Infants," 1988).

10. See Rush et al. ("Study of Infants," 1988, 487–90). WIC infants had higher mean intakes of iron (59 percent) and vitamin C (32 percent) than the comparison group. They also had significantly lower mean intakes of calcium (26 percent), protein (26 percent), and magnesium (16 percent), which reflects the fact that WIC infants were more likely to consume infant formula than whole milk. In addition to measuring mean intake, the study measured differences in the proportion of children consuming at least 77 percent of recommended dietary allowances for all nutrients. The findings were generally similar to changes in mean intakes, with 53 percent fewer WIC infants falling below that standard for iron (25.7 percent versus 54.4 percent) and 54 percent for vitamin C (9.1 percent versus 19.6 percent). Although there were no effects on the mean intake of vitamin A, WIC infants were 53 percent less likely to fall below the 77 percent recommended dietary allowance threshold than infants in the comparison group (9.8 percent versus 21 percent).

We must interpret the findings in regard to the proportion of infants with intake less than 77 percent of the recommended dietary allowance with caution, because they are based on a single twenty-four-hour recall, and measures of individual intake based on one day are subject to considerable variation.

11. See Rush et al. ("Study of Infants," 1988, 504–7).

12. See Rossi (1998, 54).

13. See Rush et al. ("Study of Infants," 1988, 484–511). WIC children ages one to five had higher mean intakes of iron (12 percent), vitamin C (13 percent), vitamin B-6 (9 percent), thiamin (8 percent), and niacin (8 percent) than the comparison group. Similarly, 14 percent fewer WIC children fell below the 77 percent recommended daily allowance for iron (62.3 versus 72.6 percent) and 22 percent less for vitamin C (21.3 versus 27.2 percent).

As mentioned above with respect to infants, we must interpret the findings regarding the proportion of children with intake less than 77 percent of the recommended daily allowance with caution, because they are based on a single twenty-four-hour recall, and measures of individual intake based on one day are subject to considerable variation.

14. See Rush et al. ("Study of Infants," 1988, 506).

15. See Rose, Habicht, and Devaney (1998).

16. The increases in iron and zinc were 16.6 and 10.6 percent of the recommended daily allowance, respectively.

17. For example, 47 percent of those receiving WIC were white, compared with 66 percent of those eligible for but not participating in WIC. Other important differences occurred in ethnicity, age of the youngest child, and geographic location.

18. See Oliveira and Gunderson (2000).

19. The authors point out that the traditional methods used to control for selection bias are based on modeling the participation process, but that the Continuing Survey of Food Intakes by Individuals did not provide sufficient information to do so. They thus resorted to an "indirect" method.

20. For example, 43 percent of the WIC sample consisted of two-year-olds versus 22 percent of those in the comparison group. There were other important differences in ethnicity, children's age, and geographic location.

21. See Yip et al. (1987).

22. See also Yip (1989) and Sherry, Bister, and Yip (1997).

23. The rate of anemia fell by over 50 percent for both groups during the study period.

24. That effect is likely because the priority system used by the program targets those with the greatest nutritional risks, and WIC expansion would generally lead to the enrollment of those with less severe nutritional problems. Sherry and her colleagues' examination of the decline in the prevalence of anemia in Vermont illustrates an example of that relationship. Although the prevalence of anemia dropped steadily from 1984 on, there was a slight increase in 1991 and 1992. The researchers noted that funding constraints led to some restrictions on eligibility in those years. They explained, "This increased the proportion of high-risk children, thus increasing the likelihood of anemia." See Sherry, Bister, and Yip (1997, 930).

25. See Devaney, Ellwood, and Love (1997, 96).

26. See Devaney (1998, 116–17). According to the General Accounting Office, about 50 percent of infant formula sold is purchased with WIC vouchers. See U.S. General Accounting Office (1998, 1).

27. In Tennessee, where information on the socioeconomic characteristics of participants was available, the prevalence of anemia declined for several different socioeconomic groups, a factor that suggests that the total decline resulted from more than just a changing composition of those covered by WIC and other public health programs.

28. See Devaney, Ellwood, and Love (1997, 95).

29. See Ohls (1998).

30. See U.S. General Accounting Office (1992).
31. See Metcoff et al. (1985). Of the 471 women who were initially enrolled, 410 completed the study.
32. See Devaney, Bilheimer, and Schore (1991).
33. WIC participants had higher birthweights, ranging from 51 grams in one state to 117 grams in another, although more significant gains were achieved for preterm births and ranged from 138 to 159 grams.
34. They estimated that WIC reduced the incidence of low-birthweight newborns from an estimated 13.6 percent without the WIC program to an estimated 9.8 percent with WIC and reduced the incidence of very low birthweight births from an estimated 3.4 percent to 1.4 percent with WIC. They derived those estimates by averaging the findings across all five states included in the study. See Devaney (1992).
35. Some of the most important health conditions related to low birthweight are cerebral palsy, deafness, blindness, and learning disabilities. See Paneth (1995).
36. See Lewit et al. (1995, 40).
37. The estimated savings to the federal government were just $1.14, with $1.04 in savings to state and local governments and $1.32 to private payers, such as hospitals and insurance companies. The savings in the first year are estimated to be $2.89 per WIC dollar spent, with savings of $.88, $.72, and $1.29 to the federal government, state and local governments, and private payers, respectively.
38. See U.S. General Accounting Office (1992, 4).
39. The GAO "statistically combined" results from seventeen studies and concluded that WIC reduced the incidence of low birthweight by 25 percent. The total effect size was estimated by weighting the evaluation effect sizes by evaluation sample size, with no apparent consideration that some studies might be more reliable than others.
40. See, for example, Devaney, Bilheimer, and Schore (1991) and Schramm (1985).

Chapter 5: Research Weaknesses

1. See Besharov, Germanis, and Rossi (1997).
2. Later in this volume, we explain that this assumption is incorrect and describe how randomized experiments can still be mounted.
3. See Gordon and Nelson (1995, 124). See also Devaney, Bilheimer, and Schore (1992, 583), who stated:

> An important caveat to these findings is that the estimated savings in Medicaid costs associated with prenatal WIC participation are not independent of any unmeasured differences between WIC participants and nonparticipants that may also influence birth outcomes and Medicaid costs. WIC participants are a self-selected group of women who

may choose to participate in the WIC program for underlying reasons that may independently lead to lower Medicaid costs. For example, some women may not participate in the WIC program because they lack access to or knowledge of publicly funded programs that provide health care or other services, which may independently affect program outcomes. Thus, the estimated savings in Medicaid costs related to prenatal WIC participation may overstate the true savings since, relative to nonparticipants, WIC participants would have lower Medicaid costs even in the absence of the WIC program. Conversely, if the WIC program is successful at reaching high-risk, low-income pregnant women, WIC participants may be more likely to have higher-cost pregnancy outcomes than nonparticipants, and estimated savings in Medicaid costs would understate the true savings associated with prenatal WIC participation.

This is how researchers at Abt Associates described the selection-bias problem:

The key methodological issue in this analysis—and, indeed, in all quasi-experimental analyses of the effects of WIC—is the noncomparability of WIC participants and eligible non-participants. When growth and health outcomes are examined for all WIC-eligible babies, differences between WIC participants and nonparticipants could be expected to arise for several reasons:

- WIC leads to better growth and health outcomes;
- regardless of the impact of WIC on growth and health outcomes, those mothers who choose to enroll their babies in WIC are women who place an especially high value on health and nutrition, and therefore they achieve better outcomes for their babies; or
- conversely, among eligibles, those women who enroll are the ones in greatest economic need, with the fewest social resources outside of the welfare system, and whose babies are at the greatest nutritional risk, and therefore they achieve worse outcomes for their babies.

See Burstein, Fox, and Puma (1991, II-9).

4. Buescher et al. (1993, 166) asserted:

The retrospective study could not control for the possible selection of more motivated women into the WIC program, except as reflected in the demographic factors incorporated into the regression analysis. Without randomization of women into WIC and non-WIC groups, there is no assurance that the two groups are comparable on other unmeasured risk factors for low birthweight. Thus, the results are subject to some degree of bias, and a causal interpretation of a WIC effect on low birthweight and costs for newborn medical care must be made with caution.

5. See Angrist and Krueger (1998, 13–14).

6. See, for example, Congress of the United States, Congressional Budget Office (1990). The National Maternal and Infant Health Survey was created specifically to study pregnancy and other outcomes. It is an unusually rich source of information (including data on smoking, alcohol consumption, and other behaviors during pregnancy), but even it does not have information on the mother's marital status or age at first birth—although it does have her current marital status.

7. See Devaney, Bilheimer, and Schore (1991, 58). Unpublished data on Medicaid savings show widely divergent findings, depending on the model used, although none were statistically significant.

8. See Devaney, Bilheimer, and Schore (1991).

9. See Rossi (1998, 57).

10. See Schramm (1986, 614). Stockbauer (1987, 817) asserted:

> This study, as well as all previous WIC studies, is retrospective in design by necessity. The confounding of self-selection is present and therefore the motivation of the two groups could be entirely different. As others have noted, the WIC group could [comprise] individuals who are more highly motivated to have a healthy baby than the non-WIC group.

11. See, for example, Rossi (1998, 58), who stated, "It appears likely that estimates uncorrected for selection biases overestimate WIC effectiveness, but the degree of overestimation cannot be reliably determined."

12. See Gordon and Nelson (1995). The survey actually included three samples of women: 9,953 mothers who experienced a live birth in 1988; 3,309 women who experienced a fetal death of at least twenty-eight weeks' gestation; and 5,332 mothers who experienced an infant death. Sample weights were used to make the combined samples representative of all births in 1988. The response rate for the survey was 74 percent for those mothers with a live birth, 65 percent for those with an infant death, and 69 percent for those with a fetal death.

13. WIC recipients were more likely than nonrecipients to be teenagers (26.6 percent versus 17.4 percent), black or Hispanic (51.8 percent versus 37.8 percent), and welfare recipients (37 percent versus 21.9 percent). They were less likely to have a high school diploma (66.5 percent versus 75 percent), to be married (48 percent versus 64.3 percent), and to have worked within the past year (54 percent versus 61.9 percent).

14. See Gordon (1993). Although that memorandum was not part of the Gordon and Nelson report, it was prepared for the U.S. Department of Agriculture to explain the methodological difficulties of adjusting for selection bias.

15. See Lopez (1999).

16. That instrument is intended to measure the variation in the availability of WIC across states, where more WIC food expenditures per capita are hypothesized to lead to greater WIC participation.

17. That instrument is intended to serve as a proxy for eligibility for public assistance, where greater family earned income is hypothesized to lead to a lower likelihood of WIC participation.
18. That instrument is intended to capture knowledge of program availability.
19. Lopez (1999, 4) asserted:

> Technically, all three methods first estimate the chances that an individual will participate in WIC based on observed characteristics and a set of variables called instruments. Usually, instruments reflect policy differences, with the main purpose of the instruments to identify the impact of policy variables which affect the chances that an individual pregnant woman participates in WIC. . . . These same instruments, however, should not influence the birth outcomes of an infant, except through the policy effects the mother faces as a result of participating in WIC. For each of these methods to work, the policy instrument must have enough variation in the provision of the policy to identify why pregnant women participate in WIC. If this does not happen, then the estimated effects, addressing selection, may not be reliable, and hence, not useful.

20. See Rossi (1998, 58).
21. Gordon first estimated the effects by using state WIC program food expenditures per capita and a variable capturing earned income as instruments. She then added a variable indicating previous WIC participation. Gordon did not have faith in those estimates, so the findings can only be found in an unpublished memorandum.
22. See Gordon (1993, 3).
23. See Fraker, Gordon, and Devaney (1995).
24. See, for example, Lopez (1999, 9), who explained that because Gordon's selection-adjusted results "are so consistent in sign (they mostly suggest negative program effects), and are statistically significant, the selection-unadjusted results . . . are likely biased up."
25. See Brien and Swann (1997, 1999b).
26. Personal communication from Michael Brien to Peter Germanis, April 20, 1999.
27. Those variables include state eligibility policies related to the self-declaration of income and use of income allowances or exemptions, the imposition of brand restrictions on food that can be purchased, the use of Aid to Families with Dependent Children eligibility for WIC eligibility, and the first-trimester hemoglobin cutoff used for nutritional risk. Other variables used include the number of WIC clinics per 1,000 poor people, the number of WIC clinics per 1,000 square miles in the state, and the generosity of each state's welfare benefits.
28. See Gordon and Nelson (1995, 104).
29. See Rossi (1998, 59).

30. See Devaney, Bilheimer, and Schore (1991).
31. Barbara L. Devaney, the principal investigator for the five-state WIC study, provided the estimates.
32. See Devaney, Bilheimer, and Schore (1992, 591–92). The benefit-cost ratios are based on the authors' calculations using data reported in the study.
33. See Devaney, Bilheimer, and Schore (1991, 54, 79). Benefit-cost ratios were calculated by using the data on Medicaid savings and WIC costs.
34. See Gordon and Nelson (1995).
35. Devaney, Bilheimer, and Schore (1991) used a thirty-six-week definition and thereby allowed more late entrants to be counted than under some of the narrower definitions used by Gordon and Nelson. The estimated effect of WIC declines with the number of months used to define participation. For example, using an eight-month definition suggests an impact of 53 grams on mean birthweight, whereas a six-month definition leads to an impact of just 10 grams, which is not statistically significant.
36. That differs from the second approach in that for each cohort, all women had pregnancies lasting at least the specified number of weeks. For example, for the twenty-eight-week cohort, all women who enrolled during the first six months are counted as WIC participants, and all those who did not are in the comparison group. For the forty-week cohort, only pregnancies lasting at least nine months are counted. Thus, the sample size (and the sample's representativeness of the broader WIC population) diminishes as the time frame is extended. For purposes of adjusting for simultaneity bias, however, the shorter cohorts are more important. No statistically significant birthweight effects were found by using that approach.
37. See Gordon and Nelson (1995, xvii).
38. Ibid., 112. Women who enrolled in WIC after the sixth month are classified as nonparticipants. This may understate the impact of WIC, because those who enroll later in the pregnancies may nevertheless benefit from WIC, but they are included in the comparison group rather than in the treatment group.
39. See Ahluwalia et al. (1998).
40. Ibid., 1376.
41. See Rossi (1998, 59).
42. See Devaney and Schirm (1993).
43. See Rossi (1998, 167).
44. See Gordon and Nelson (1995, xvii). Other smaller differences in estimated effects on birth outcomes existed between the two studies, with the Devaney (1992) study generally showing both a larger incidence of adverse birth outcomes and a larger WIC effect.
45. See Rossi (1998, 90).
46. See Gordon (1993, 19).
47. See Devaney, Bilheimer, and Schore (1992, 591–92).
48. See Devaney, Bilheimer, and Schore (1990, 63).

Chapter 6: Does WIC "Work"?

1. Compare that with Rossi (1998, 90), who stated, "The research in question is of high quality, and results from the several independently conducted studies are largely consistent."
2. See Rush et al. ("Study of Infants," 1988, 484–511).
3. See Gordon and Nelson (1995).
4. See Brien and Swann (1999b).
5. Ibid.
6. See Goldenberg and Rouse (1998, 315).
7. Rossi (1998, 63) stated, "Although WIC benefits are less in dollar value and of limited duration, the question may be raised whether the vouchers simply replace ordinary income resulting in no significant change in food purchasing amount or quality or whether the vouchers significantly alter food purchasing patterns in the desired direction."
8. See Arcia, Crouch, and Kulka (1990).
9. See U.S. General Accounting Office (1999).
10. See, for example, Paneth (1995, 21), Alexander and Korenbrot (1995, 109), and Susser (1991).
11. See Mathews et al. (1999).
12. See Shiono and Behrman (1995, 12).
13. See Alexander and Korenbrot (1995, 109).
14. Ibid., 104.
15. See Moreno et al. (1997). We should interpret those disappointing findings with caution. First, the evaluation design, also not a randomized experiment, compares birth outcomes in Healthy Start communities and those in similar communities not participating in the program. The Healthy Start and comparison sites were matched on a limited number of variables, and many differences among the sites may confound the findings. Moreover, the effectiveness in implementing the projects varied across the sites, and that could have "made the difference between successful and less-than-successful implementation." Nevertheless, Healthy Start spends an average of $146 per month for each maternal participant—more than three times as much as WIC. Hence, one would have expected Healthy Start to do at least as well as WIC—if the WIC findings are valid.

Second, Healthy Start is not exactly WIC. WIC could be considered primarily a nutrition program that provides food benefits, directed counseling, and referrals. In contrast, Healthy Start could be considered mainly a health program that focuses primarily on outreach and case management services. Both programs, however, share similar objectives and provide many of the same services, primarily nutrition education and referral to other health and social services. In addition, many Healthy Start grantees are also WIC providers, and, if anything, the Healthy Start program (except for the nutrition supplements) is an enriched version of WIC.

16. See Devaney, Bilheimer, and Schore (1992, 591–92). The benefit-cost ratios are based on the authors' calculations using data reported in the study.

17. The benefit-cost findings are based on three following assumptions. First, WIC reduces the incidence of low birthweight by one percentage point for whites and between four and seven percentage points for blacks. Second, the cost of a low birthweight baby is $15,000. Third, the average cost per WIC participant is $233. Those assumptions are derived from Brien and Swann's own research and other data on WIC expenditures and costs associated with low birthweight.

18. See Brien and Swann (1999b, 26). Their results for whites suggest that WIC saves $.64 for each dollar spent.

19. See Watkins (1998).

20. See Center on Budget and Policy Priorities (1997, 6).

21. See U.S. General Accounting Office (1992, 43).

22. See U.S. General Accounting Office (1997a, 10).

23. Ibid.

24. See RAND Corporation (1998).

25. See Karoly et al. (1998, xviii–xix).

26. Quoted in Rush et al. ("Background," 1988, 45). See also Rossi (1998, 45).

27. See http://www.shapeup.org/general/koop.htm.

28. See National Center for Health Statistics (2001b). See also Kuczmarski et al. (1994) and Borrud, Enns, and Mickle (1996). Using the broader definition of *overweight* recommended by the American Heart Association "results in over half of all adults being classified as overweight in 1988–1994." See Frazao (1999, 14). That definition was based on research that mortality rates increased substantially for those with a "body mass index" greater than twenty-five. The body mass index is calculated as weight in kilograms divided by height in meters squared (kg/m^2).

    More recent trends suggest that the prevalence of obesity has continued to worsen in the 1990s. Using a differently calibrated measure, another group of researchers found that the prevalence of obesity increased from 12 percent in 1991 to 17.9 percent in 1998. See Mokdad et al. (1999).

29. See National Center for Health Statistics (2001a).

30. See National Center for Health Statistics (2001a), Mei et al. (1998), Ogden et al. (1997), and Troiano et al. (1995).

31. *Overweight* was defined by the age- and sex-specific eighty-fifth percentile of body mass index. See Troiano et al. (1995, 1085). When the ninety-fifth percentile is used, the prevalence of overweight declines to 10.9 percent. The trend in the prevalence of overweight among children, however, is comparable using either criterion. See Hamilton et al. (1997, 48). According to the definition used, "households with children have reduced the children's food intake to an extent that it implies that children have experienced the physical sensation of hunger." The USDA has published data on food security through 1998, including an estimate that 4.8 percent of children lived

in households that experienced food insecurity "great enough that one or more household members were hungry at least some time during the period due to inadequate resources for food." But the report cautioned:

> [T]he measure of children in food-insecure households with hunger is not, as such, a valid estimate of the number of children directly experiencing hunger, but a rather wide upper-bound for this figure. In most households, children present are shielded from food deprivation until the level of deprivation among adult members is quite severe. Work is currently underway to develop a more accurate estimate of children's hunger from the CPS data.

See Bickel, Carlson, and Nord (1999, 1, 13).

32. See Galuska et al. (1996), U.S. Department of Health and Human Services, Centers for Disease Control, National Center for Health Statistics (1999), and "Profile of Overweight Children" (1999).

33. That definition of *hunger* reflects a "social" rather than a "medical" problem. The 1984 President's Task Force on Hunger linked medical definitions of *hunger* to "a weakened, disordered condition brought about by prolonged lack of food" that was associated with conditions such as serious underweight or stunting of growth in children. In contrast, hunger as a social problem was defined as "a situation in which someone cannot obtain an adequate amount of food, even if the shortage is not prolonged enough to cause health problems." See Hamilton et al. (1997, 3).

34. See Hamilton et al. (1997, viii–ix).

35. See "Facts about Childhood Obesity and Overweightness" (1999).

36. See Glickman (1998).

37. See Devaney (1997, 16). She reported that "between one quarter and one half of low-income [WIC] eligible individuals selected by even fairly generous cutoff value are at risk of being overweight" (p. 25).

38. See Troiano et al. (1995, 1085). See also Calle et al. (1999), Must et al. (1999), and Allison et al. (1999).

39. See Hedberg, Bracken, and Stashwick (1999, 141).

40. See Hill and Trowbridge (1998, 570).

Chapter 7: Programmatic Flexibility

1. For example, although one of the primary objectives of the New Chance Demonstration was to reduce subsequent childbearing, over 7 percent more New Chance mothers experienced a pregnancy than those randomly assigned to a control group (57 percent versus 53 percent). See Quint et al. (1994).

2. See the National Association of WIC Directors' Web site at http://www.wicdirectors.org/legagenda8.htm.

3. Those are the authors' calculations, based on U.S. Department of Agriculture and Census data.

4. See U.S. General Accounting Office (1998, 1).
5. See Ku, Cohen, and Pindus (1994, 8).
6. See Institute of Medicine (1996, 8).
7. See Whaley and True (2000).
8. See Contento (1995, 331).
9. Ibid.
10. See Schiller and Fox (1999).
11. See Whaley and True (2000, 8).
12. See Troiano (1995, 1090).
13. See Galuska et al. (1996, 1729) and Kuczmarski et al. (1994, 209).
14. See Glickman (1998).
15. See Ogden et al. (1997).
16. See Mei et al. (1998), Ogden et al.(1997), and Troiano et al. (1995).
17. See Contento (1995, 298–99).
18. Ibid.
19. See Schiller and Fox (1999).
20. See Contento (1995, 356–57). That issue summarized studies "with strong evaluation designs," including those involving random assignment and strong quasi-experimental designs. A summary of that synthesis appears in Schiller and Fox (1999).
21. Schiller and Fox (1999) summarized the research in Contento (1995).
22. See Burkhead et al. (1995, 312–16).
23. See, for example, Mead (1997).
24. See Long and Bos (1998).
25. See Kerpelman et al. (1999).
26. See Olds et al. (1997).
27. See Whaley and True (2000, 8).
28. Scc Epstein (1999).
29. Personal communication with Alan Kendal, April 1, 1999.
30. See Ku, Cohen, and Pindus (1994, 19).
31. See Whaley and True (2000, 15).

Chapter 8: Rigorous Evaluation

1. See Olds et al. (1997, 641).
2. See Bos and Fellerath (1997, 38).
3. See Puma, Burstein, and Fox (1992, vi).
4. See Lopez (1999).
5. See Brien and Swann (1997, 1999b).
6. See Besharov, Germanis, and Rossi (1997, 42).
7. See U.S. General Accounting Office (1997a, 15).
8. See Ku, Cohen, and Pindus (1994, 6).
9. Moreover, that proportion may decline in the near future, because the number of potentially eligible children has been expanded by recent Medicaid

expansions, which increasingly include children in families with incomes above 185 percent of poverty (the WIC income maximum).

10. Although we do not have estimates of the number of children eligible by age, the number of children participating declines rapidly as children grow older. For example, in 1996, 1.4 million one-year-olds participated in WIC, compared with 1 million two-year-olds, 900,000 three-year-olds, and just 600,000 four-year-olds. See Randall, Bartlett, and Kennedy (1998, 36). That drop in participation is surely much more rapid than the decline in the number of eligible children and suggests that perhaps as few as one-third of income-eligible four-year-olds participate in the program.

11. See U.S. General Accounting Office (1997a, 15).

12. See Advisory Committee on Head Start Research and Evaluation (1999, vii).

13. Program coverage for pregnant women should be expected to be below 100 percent, because women are unlikely to participate for the full forty weeks of pregnancy. Thus, it is unlikely that the 69 percent coverage rate estimated in 1997 can be significantly increased.

14. See Rossi (1998, 101).

15. See U.S. General Accounting Office (1997a, 15).

16. See Orr (1998, part 5, 13). See also Puma et al. (1991).

Chapter 9: Conclusion

1. Besharov remembers when, as late as the early 1970s, many low-income mothers would sell the infant formula given them so that they would have more cash. With the current flood of infant formula in most poor neighborhoods, no market for the resale of infant formula exists, so formula is now much more likely to be given to newborns.

Appendix: Attempting to Correct for Selection Bias

1. Brien and Swann (1997, 1999b). The 1999 paper is a revision of the 1997 paper, rather than a separate study. We examine both papers to show the sensitivity of the findings to differences in sample selection and methodology.

2. Personal communication from Peter H. Rossi to Douglas J. Besharov, March 25, 1999.

3. Brien and Swann (1997).

4. Hispanics were excluded because of small sample sizes and to allow the researchers to analyze "homogeneous" groups.

5. Brien and Swann (1999b).

6. Of course, that also increased the likelihood of including ineligible individuals in the eligible nonparticipant group.

7. Personal communication from Michael Brien to Peter Germanis, December 15, 1999.

8. The modifications to the sample resulted in a considerable change in sample sizes among the various groups, with corresponding changes in their char-

acteristics. For example, expanding the definition of WIC increased the sample size of white WIC participants from 562 to 967 and the sample size of black participants from 2,018 to 3,188. Adding the infant death sample was one factor in increasing the sample size, but because the data were "weighted," they were still representative of all births in 1988. Another factor influencing the size of the sample was the inclusion of previously ineligible groups, which tended to make both the WIC and the comparison groups somewhat less disadvantaged on a range of characteristics.

9. Personal communication from Michael J. Brien to Peter Germanis, April 20, 1999.

10. The variables include adequacy of prenatal care; whether the mother smoked, drank alcohol, or used drugs; whether she worked during pregnancy; whether she was under age twenty or over age thirty-five; whether her income was between zero and $5,000, between $5,000 and $10,000, or between $10,000 and $20,000; whether she was married; whether she lived with the child's father; and whether she lived with either of her parents.

11. Those variables include whether the mother worked during pregnancy; whether she was under age eighteen or over age thirty-four; whether her income was between zero and $5,000, between $5,000 and $10,000, or between $10,000 and $20,000; whether she was married; whether she lived with the child's father; and whether she lived with her parents.

12. The behavioral variables include whether the mother was underweight; whether she was obese; her weight before pregnancy; her level of prenatal care; and whether she smoked, drank alcohol, or used drugs.

13. Brien and Swann used the basic model for those attempts because of concerns about the "endogeneity of the demographic and behavioral variables."

14. The 1999 study had the infant death sample, which included a live birth that was followed by an infant death.

15. Personal communication from Michael Brien to Peter Germanis, April 20, 1999.

16. The mean incidence of low birthweight is not reported for women with two or more births, so the percent reduction is approximated by using the mean for all women in the sample.

17. Brien and Swann (1999b, 26–28).

PART TWO
Chapter 10: Addressing the Selection-Bias Problem for Program Targeting and Design

1. Selection bias exists if WIC participants are either healthier or less healthy than eligible nonparticipants in unobserved ways.

2. See Brien and Swann (1999b).

3. See Brien and Swann (1999a).

4. For the child health project, data limitations preclude the use of fixed effects.

5. Regarding the last point, we note that other researchers have not found large effects of other programs considered by themselves. See Currie and Cole (1993) and Kaestner, Yazici, and Joyce (1997).
6. See Brien and Swann (1999a).

Chapter 11: An Incremental Approach to Testing WIC's Efficacy

1. See LaLonde and Maynard (1987).
2. See, for example, Devaney, Bilheimer, and Schore (1990), Devaney and Schirm (1993), Gordon and Nelson (1995), and Burstein, Fox, and Puma (1991).
3. See Gordon and Nelson (1995, 125).
4. See Metcoff et al. (1985).
5. If WIC vouchers for infant formula were converted to food stamps on a national basis, taxpayer expense would clearly be increased because of the lost rebate from formula manufacturers. I for one would deem that a worthwhile change. It is hard to defend the government's using its monopsony power to extract an involuntary program subsidy from an industry.

Chapter 12: A Defense of the Existing Research on WIC

1. See Rossi (1998, 54).
2. See Rush et al. ("Study Methodology," 1988, 437).
3. See Rose, Habicht, and Devaney (1998).
4. See Devaney, Bilheimer, and Schore (1992), Gordon and Nelson (1995), Kennedy et al. (1982), Kotelchuck et al. (1984), and Ahluwalia et al. (1998).
5. See Rush et al. ("Study of Infants," 1988) and Rose, Habicht, and Devaney (1998).
6. See Beaton (1999) and Institute of Medicine (2000).
7. See Yip et al. (1987).

Chapter 13: Enhancing WIC's Effectiveness

1. See Besharov and Germanis (1999, 114).
2. A few floor statements mistakenly applied the three-to-one ratio to the program as a whole, but they were not made by members who were key policymakers. It is not uncommon for a staffer writing a floor statement for a member who is not a key policymaker on the legislative matter at hand and who is not intimately involved with the particular program—or provision of the tax code—in question to misstate some information relating to the program or tax provision. For probably few, if any, major programs, tax provisions, or pieces of legislation has that not occurred.
3. On one occasion, an internal newsletter of the U.S. Department of Agriculture's Food and Nutrition Service evidently was not properly reviewed

and misapplied the savings ratio. But that was the exception, not the rule. The Food and Nutrition Service has produced countless documents on WIC over the past two decades that have applied the savings ratio correctly.

4. Besharov and Germanis quote selectively from the Urban Institute review in a few places where the quotation supports a point they make, but they do not report that the review as a whole disagrees substantially with their presentation of the research findings.

5. See Yip et al. (1987, 1621).

6. The Centers for Disease Control research found that differences in anemia rates between children at initial WIC enrollment and children at follow-up visits narrowed over time, apparently because of reductions over time in the anemia rates of children entering WIC. The WIC program would be expected to have more dramatic effects in lowering child anemia rates when anemia rates among children entering the program are high than when anemia rates among such children are lower.

7. See Rose, Habicht, and Devaney (1998).

8. See Devaney et al. (2000).

9. See Ku (1999, 110).

10. Besharov and Germanis argue that Medicaid expansions will cause WIC participation to rise, but such expansions have occurred in the period since 1996, during which WIC participation has failed to increase.

11. See Sigma One Corporation (2000).

12. Alternatively, it could be said that the principal use of rebate savings today is to sustain participation—in other words, that without rebates, WIC participation would be much lower. I think, however, that Congress and the executive branch are unlikely to allow WIC participation to plunge if infant formula cost containment somehow collapsed. It is more likely that they would appropriate additional funds to avoid sharp cutbacks in WIC participation.

13. See U.S. Department of Agriculture, Food and Nutrition Service, Office of Analysis and Evaluation (2000b).

14. Two-thirds of the growth between fiscal year 1992 and fiscal year 1997, when WIC participation hit its peak, occurred among children.

15. See Gordon et al. (1999).

16. In calling for changes in the WIC eligibility criteria, Besharov and Germanis cite an Institute of Medicine report questioning some WIC eligibility practices. It may not be clear from Besharov and Germanis's treatment of that issue, but the Institute of Medicine report focused on the WIC nutritional eligibility criteria, not the income limits. Furthermore, the changes in the WIC nutritional risk criteria that the USDA instituted in April 1999 were designed in significant part in response to the Institute of Medicine's concerns.

17. That the USDA would have to approve waivers seeking to add foods to the WIC food packages does not provide sufficient protection. State politicians and members of Congress from a state seeking such a waiver, as well as the

segment of the food industry in question, would likely press the USDA to approve the waiver. Standing up to pressure related to a waiver request from a particular state would be harder for the USDA than standing up to pressure to alter the national WIC food packages.

References

References

Advisory Committee on Head Start Research and Evaluation. 1999. *Evaluating Head Start: A Recommended Framework for Studying the Impact of the Head Start Program.* Washington, D.C.: U.S. Department of Health and Human Services, October.

Ahluwalia, Indu B., Vijaya K. Hogan, Lawrence Grummer-Strawn, William R. Colville, and Alwin Peterson. 1998. "The Effect of WIC Participation on Small-for-Gestational-Age Births: Michigan, 1992." *American Journal of Public Health* 88 (9): 1374–77.

Alexander, Greg R., and Carol S. Korenbrot. 1995. "The Role of Prenatal Care in Preventing Low Birth Weight." *Future of Children* 5 (1): 103–20.

Allison, David B., Kevin R. Fontaine, JoAnn E. Manson, June Stevens, and Theodore B. Van Itallie. 1999. "Annual Deaths Attributable to Obesity in the United States." *Journal of the American Medical Association* 282 (16): 1530–38.

Angrist, Joshua D., and Alan B. Krueger. 1998. "Empirical Strategies in Labor Economics." Working Paper No. 401, Princeton University.

Arcia, Gustavo J., Luis A. Crouch, and Richard A. Kulka. 1990. "Impact of the WIC Program on Food Expenditures." *American Journal of Agricultural Economics* 72 (1): 218–26.

Beaton, G. H. 1999. "Recommended Dietary Intakes: Individuals and Populations." In M. E. Shils, J. A. Olson, M. Shike, and A. C. Ross, eds., *Modern Nutrition in Health and Disease*, 9th ed. Baltimore, Md.: Williams and Wilkins.

Besharov, Douglas J., and Peter Germanis. 1999. "A Reply." *Public Interest*, no. 135 (Spring): 114.

Besharov, Douglas J., Peter Germanis, and Peter H. Rossi. 1997. *Evaluating Welfare Reform: A Guide for Scholars and Practitioners.* College Park, Md.: University of Maryland School of Public Affairs.

Bickel, Gary, Steven Carlson, and Mark Nord. 1999. *Household Food Security in the United States, 1995–1998: Advance Report.* Alexandria, Va.: U.S. Department of Agriculture, Food and Nutrition Service, Office of Analysis, Nutrition, and Evaluation.

Borrud, Lori, Cecilia Wilkinson Enns, and Sharon Mickle. 1996. "USDA Surveys Food Consumption Changes." *Food Review* (September–December 1996): 14–19.

Bos, Johannes M., and Veronica Fellerath. 1997. *Final Report on Ohio's Welfare Initiative to Improve School Attendance among Teenage Parents: Ohio's Learning, Earning, and Parenting Program.* New York: Manpower Demonstration Research Corporation, August.

Brien, Michael J., and Christopher A. Swann. 1997. "Prenatal WIC Participation and Infant Health: Selection and Maternal Fixed Effects." Discussion Paper 295, Thomas Jefferson Center, University of Virginia.

———. 1999a. "Government Intervention and Health: The Impact of WIC Participation on Children." University of Virginia.

———. 1999b. "Prenatal WIC Participation and Infant Health: Selection and Maternal Fixed Effects." University of Virginia.

Buescher, Paul A., Linnea C. Larson, M. D. Nelson, Jr., and Alice J. Lenihan. 1993. "Prenatal WIC Participation Can Reduce Low Birth Weight and Newborn Medical Costs: A Cost-Benefit Analysis of WIC Participation in North Carolina." *Journal of the American Dietetic Association* 93 (2): 163–66.

Burkhead, Guthrie S., Charles W. LeBaron, Patricia Parsons, John C. Grabau, Linda Barr-Gale, John Fuhrman, Steven Brooks, Jorge Rosenthal, Stephen C. Hadler, and Dale L. Morse. 1995. "The Immunization of Children Enrolled in the Special Supplemental Food Program for Women, Infants, and Children (WIC): The Impact of Different Strategies." *Journal of the American Medical Association* 274 (4): 312–16.

Burstein, Nancy, Mary Kay Fox, Michael J. Puma. 1991. *Study of the Impact of WIC on the Growth and Development of Children: Field Test. Volume II: Preliminary Impact Estimates.* Cambridge, Mass.: Abt Associates.

Caan, Bette, Donna M. Horgen, Sheldon Margen, Janet C. King, and Nicholas P. Jewell. 1987. "Benefits Associated with WIC Supplemental Feeding during the Interpregnancy Interval." *American Journal of Clinical Nutrition* 45: 29–41.

Calle, Eugenia E., Michael J. Thun, Jennifer M. Petrelli, Carmen Rodriguez, and Clark W. Heath, Jr. 1999. "Body-Mass Index and Mortality in a Prospective Cohort of U.S. Adults." *New England Journal of Medicine* 341 (15): 1097–1105.

Center on Budget and Policy Priorities. 1997. "WIC Program Faces Caseload Reductions in Coming Months Unless Supplemental Funding Is Provided." May 3.

Congress of the United States, Congressional Budget Office. 1990. *Sources of Support for Adolescent Mothers.* Washington, D.C.: Government Printing Office.

Contento, Isobel. 1995. "Nutrition Education for Pregnant Women and Care-takers of Infants." *Journal of Nutrition Education* 27 (6).

Currie, Janet, and Nancy Cole. 1993. "Welfare and Child Health: The Link between AFDC Participation and Birth Weight." *American Economic Review* 83 (3):971–85.

Devaney, Barbara L. 1992. *Very Low Birthweight among Medicaid Newborns in Five States: The Effects of Prenatal WIC Participation.* Alexandria, Va.: U.S. Department of Agriculture, Food and Nutrition Service.

————. 1997. *Yield of Risk for Three WIC Nutrition Risk Criteria.* Princeton, N.J.: Mathematica Policy Research.

————. 1998. "Comments on the WIC Program." In Peter H. Rossi, *Feeding the Poor: Assessing Federal Food Aid.* Washington, D.C.: AEI Press, 1998.

Devaney, Barbara L., and Allen Schirm. 1993. *Infant Mortality among Medicaid Newborns in Five States: The Effects of Prenatal WIC Participation.* Alexandria, Va.: U.S. Department of Agriculture, Food and Nutrition Service.

Devaney, Barbara L., Linda Bilheimer, and Jennifer Schore. 1990. *The Savings in Medicaid Costs for Newborns and Their Mothers from Prenatal Participation in the WIC Program,* vol. 1. Alexandria, Va.: U.S. Department of Agriculture, Food and Nutrition Service.

————. 1991. *The Savings in Medicaid Costs for Newborns and Their Mothers from Prenatal Participation in the WIC Program,* vol. 2. Alexandria, Va.: U.S. Department of Agriculture, Food and Nutrition Service.

————. 1992. "Medicaid Costs and Birth Outcomes: The Effects of Prenatal WIC Participation and the Use of Prenatal Care." *Journal of Policy Analysis and Management* 11 (4): 573–92.

Devaney, Barbara L., Marilyn R. Ellwood, and John M. Love. 1997. "Programs That Mitigate the Effects of Poverty on Children." *Future of Children* 7 (2): 88–112.

Devaney, Barbara L., Embry Howell, Marie McCormick, and Lorenzo Moreno. 2000. *Reducing Infant Mortality: Lessons Learned from Healthy Start: Final Report.* Princeton, N.J.: Mathematica Policy Research, July.

Epstein, Jodie Levin, Center for Law and Social Policy. 1999. Memorandum to Phoebe Cottingham, Smith-Richardson Foundation. June 16.

"Facts about Childhood Obesity and Overweightness." 1999. *Family Economic and Nutrition Review* 12 (1): 52–53.

Fox, Mary Kay, Nancy Burstein, Jenny Golay, and Cristofer Price. 1999. *WIC Nutrition Education Assessment Study: Final Report.* Alexandria, Va.: U.S. Department of Agriculture, Food and Nutrition Service.

Fraker, Thomas M., Anne R. Gordon, and Barbara L. Devaney. 1995. "The Use of Selection-Bias Models in Program Evaluation." Washington, D.C.: Mathematica Policy Research.

Frazao, Elizabeth. 1999. "High Costs of Poor Eating Patterns in the United States." In Elizabeth Frazao, ed., *America's Eating Habits: Changes and Consequences.* Washington, D.C.: U.S. Department of Agriculture, Economic Research Service.

Galuska, Deborah A., Mary Serdula, Elsie Pamuk, Paul Z. Siegel, and Tim Byers. 1996. "Trends in Overweight among U.S. Adults from 1987 to 1993: A Multistate Telephone Survey." *American Journal of Public Health* 86 (12): 1729–35.

Glickman, Dan. 1997. USDA press conference on Women, Infants, and Children Program. May 13.

———. 1998. "Remarks." USDA Symposium on Childhood Obesity: Causes and Prevention. October 27.

Goldenberg, Robert L., and Dwight Rouse. 1998. "Prevention of Premature Birth." *New England Journal of Medicine* 339 (5): 313–20.

Gordon, Anne R. 1993. Memorandum to Janet Tognetti. "Effects of Prenatal WIC Participation on Birth Outcomes Estimated Using Alternative Selection-Bias Correction Methods." Princeton, N.J.: Mathematica Policy Research, June 9.

Gordon, Anne R., and Lyle Nelson. 1995. *Characteristics and Outcomes of WIC Participants and Nonparticipants: Analysis of the 1988 National Maternal and Infant Health Survey.* Alexandria, Va.: U.S. Department of Agriculture, Food and Nutrition Service.

Gordon, Anne R., Rebecca Kliman, Jim Ohls, Jacqueline Anderson, and Kristin LaBounty. 1999. *Estimating the Number of People Eligible for WIC and the Full-Funding Participation Rate: A Review of the Issues.* Princeton, N.J.: Mathematica Policy Research, February.

Hamilton, William L., John T. Cook, William W. Thompson, Lawrence F. Burton, Edward A. Frongillo, Jr., Christine M. Olson, and Cheryl A. Wehler. 1997. *Household Food Security in the United States in 1995.* Cambridge, Mass.: Abt Associates.

Hedberg, Viking A., Ann C. Bracken, and Carole A. Stashwick. 1999. "Long-Term Consequences of Adolescent Health Behaviors: Implications for Adolescent Health Services." *Adolescent Medicine* 10 (1): 137–51.

Hill, James O., and Frederick L. Trowbridge. 1998. "Childhood Obesity: Future Directions and Research Priorities." *Pediatrics* 101 (3): 570.

Huntington, Jane, and Frederick A. Connell. 1994. "For Every Dollar Spent—The Cost-Savings Argument for Prenatal Care." *New England Journal of Medicine* 331 (19): 1306–7.

Institute of Medicine. 1996. *WIC Nutrition Risk Criteria: A Scientific Assessment.* Washington, D.C.: National Academy Press.

———. 2000. *Dietary Reference Intakes: Applications in Dietary Assessment.* Washington, D.C.: National Academy Press.

Kaestner, R., E. Yazici, and T. Joyce. 1997. "Does Medicaid Improve Infant and Child Health?" Paper presented at the annual meeting of the Population Association of America. Washington, D.C.

Karoly, Lynn A., Peter W. Greenwood, Susan S. Everingham, Jill Hoube, M. Rebecca Kilburn, C. Peter Rydell, Matthew Sanders, and James Chisea. 1998. *Investing in Our Children: What We Know and Don't Know About the*

Costs and Benefits of Early Childhood Interventions. Santa Monica, Calif.: RAND Corporation.

Kennedy, Eileen T., Stanley Gershoff, Robert Reed, and James E. Austin. 1982. "Evaluation of the Effect of WIC Supplemental Feeding on Birth Weight." *Journal of the American Dietetic Association* 80 (March): 220–27.

Kerpelman, Larry C., David P. Connell, Walter Gunn, Robert Schmitz, and Jonathan Wilwerding. 1999. *Preschool Immunization Project Evaluation: Executive Summary.* Cambridge, Mass.: Abt Associates.

Kotelchuck, Milton, Janet B. Schwartz, Marlene T. Anderka, and Karl S. Finison. 1984. "WIC Participation and Pregnancy Outcomes: Massachusetts Statewide Evaluation Project." *American Journal of Public Health* 74 (10): 1086–92.

Kramer-LeBlanc, Carol S., Anne Mardis, Shirley Gerrior, and Nancy Gaston. 1999. *Review of the Nutritional Status of WIC Participants.* Washington, D.C.: U.S. Department of Agriculture, Center for Nutrition Policy and Promotion.

Krause, Mara. 1999. "States Have Expanded Eligibility through Medicaid and the State Children's Health Insurance Program." Washington, D.C.: NGA Center for Best Practices, Health Policy Studies Division, February 10.

Ku, Leighton. 1999. "Debating WIC." *Public Interest,* no. 135 (Spring): 108–12.

Ku, Leighton, Barbara Cohen, and Nancy Pindus. 1994. *Full Funding for WIC: A Policy Review.* Washington, D.C.: Urban Institute.

Kuczmarski, Robert J., Katherine M. Flegal, Stephen M. Campbell, and Clifford Johnson. 1994. "Increasing Prevalence of Overweight among U.S. Adults: The National Health and Nutrition Examination Surveys, 1960 to 1991." *Journal of the American Medical Association* 272 (3): 205–11.

LaLonde, R., and R. Maynard. 1987. "How Precise Are Evaluations of Employment and Training Programs? Evidence from a Field Experiment." *Evaluation Review* 11 (4): 428–51.

Lewis, Kimball, and Marilyn Ellwood. 1998. *Medicaid Policies and Eligibility for WIC.* Cambridge, Mass.: Mathematica Policy Research.

Lewit, Eugene M., Linda S. Baker, Hope Corman, and Patricia H. Shiono. 1995. "The Direct Cost of Low Birth Weight." *Future of Children* 5 (1): 35–56.

Long, David A., and Johannes M. Bos. 1998. *Learnfare: How to Implement a Mandatory Stay-in-School Program for Teenage Parents on Welfare.* New York: Manpower Demonstration Research Corporation.

Lopez, Mark Hugo. 1999. "Evaluating WIC: Comments on Recent Research." University of Maryland School of Public Affairs. March.

Macro International, Inc., and Urban Institute. 1995. *Final Report—WIC Dynamics,* vol. 1. Alexandria, Va.: U.S. Department of Agriculture, Food and Consumer Service.

Martin, Joyce A., Betty L. Smith, T. J. Mathews, and Stephanie J. Ventura. 1999. "Births and Deaths: Preliminary Data for 1998." *National Vital Statistics Reports.* Hyattsville, Md.: U.S. Department of Health and Human Services, Centers for Disease Control, National Center for Health Statistics.

Mathews, Fiona, et al. 1999. "Influence of Maternal Nutrition on Outcome of Pregnancy: Prospective Cohort Study." *British Medical Journal* 319 (August 7): 339–43.

Mead, Lawrence M. 1997. *The New Paternalism: Supervisory Approaches to Poverty.* Washington, D.C.: Brookings Institution.

Mei, Zuguo, Kelly S. Scanlon, Laurence M. Grummer-Strawn, David S. Freedman, Ray Yip, and Frederick L. Trowbridge. 1998. "Increasing Prevalence of Overweight among U.S. Low-Income Preschool Children: The Centers for Disease Control and Prevention Pediatric Nutrition Surveillance, 1983 to 1995." *Pediatrics* 101 (1): 1–6.

Metcoff, James, Paul Costiloe, Warren M. Crosby, Seshachalam Dutta, Harold H. Sandstead, David Milne, C. E. Bodwell, and Stephen H. Majors. 1985. "Effect of Food Supplementation (WIC) during Pregnancy on Birth Weight." *American Journal of Clinical Nutrition* 41 (May): 933–47.

Miller, Susan. 1999. "Reinventing Nutrition Education in WIC." Discussion paper based on an April 1999 meeting of the National Association of WIC Directors. New Orleans, La. June 22.

Mokdad, Ali H., Mary K. Serdula, William H. Dietz, Barbara A. Bowman, James S. Marks, and Jeffrey P. Koplan. 1999. "The Spread of the Obesity Epidemic in the United States, 1991–1998." *Journal of the American Medical Association* 282 (16): 1519–22.

Moreno, Lorenzo, Barbara L. Devaney, Dexter Chu, Catherine Brown, Marie McCormick, and Embry Howell. 1997. *Interim Findings: Impact of Healthy Start on Infant Mortality and Other Birth Outcomes.* Princeton, N.J.: Mathematica Policy Research.

Must, Aviva, Jennifer Spadano, Eugenie H. Coakley, Aliso E. Field, Graham Colditz, and William H. Dietz. 1999. "The Disease Burden Associated with Overweight and Obesity." *Journal of the American Medical Association* 282 (16): 1523–29.

National Center for Health Statistics. 2001a. *Prevalence of Overweight among Children and Adolescents: United States, 1999.* Hyattsville, Md.: National Center for Health Statistics.

———. 2001b. *Prevalence of Overweight and Obesity among Adults: United States, 1999.* Hyattsville, Md.: National Center for Health Statistics.

Ogden, Cynthia L., Richard P. Troiano, Ronette R. Briefel, Robert Kuczmarski, Katherine M. Flegal, and Clifford L. Johnson. 1997. "Prevalence of Overweight among Preschool Children in the United States, 1971 through 1994." *Pediatrics* 99 (4).

Ohls, James. 1998. "Remarks." In National Research Council, *Workshop on Evaluation of Food Assistance Programs in an Era of Welfare Reform: Background Materials,* February 12–13.

Olds, David, John Eckenrode, Charles R. Henderson, Harriet Kitzman, Jane Powers, Robert Cole, Kimberly Sidora, Pamela Morris, Lisa Pettitt, and Dennis Luckey. 1997. "Long-Term Effects of Home Visitation on Maternal

Life Course and Child Abuse and Neglect: Fifteen-Year Follow-Up of a Randomized Trial." *Journal of the American Medical Association* 278 (8): 637–43.

Oliveira, Victor, and Craig Gunderson. 2000. "WIC and the Nutrient Intake of Children." Food Assistance and Nutrition Research Report No. 5. Washington, D.C.: U.S. Department of Agriculture, Economic Research Service. March.

Orr, Larry. 1998. "Implementation and Data Collection." In Larry Orr, *Social Experimentation: Evaluating Public Programs with Experimental Methods.* Washington, D.C.: U.S. Department of Health and Human Services, Office of the Assistant Secretary for Planning and Evaluation.

Paneth, Nigel S. 1995. "The Problem of Low Birthweight." *Future of Children* 5 (1): 19–34.

"Profile of Overweight Children." 1999. *Nutrition Insights* 13 (May): 1–2.

Puma, Michael J., Nancy R. Burstein, and Mary Kay Fox. 1992. *Study of the Impact of WIC on the Growth and Development of Children: A Field Test.* Cambridge, Mass.: Abt Associates.

Puma, Michael J., Janet DiPietro, Jeanne Rosenthal, David Connell, David Judkins, and Mary Kay Fox. 1991. *Study of the Impact of WIC on the Growth and Development of Children. Field Test: Feasibility Assessment. Final Report,* vol. 1. Cambridge, Mass.: Abt Associates.

Quint, Janet, Denise Polit, Hans Bos, and George Cave. 1994. *New Chance: Interim Findings on a Comprehensive Program for Disadvantaged Young Mothers and Their Children.* New York, N.Y.: Manpower Demonstration Research Corporation.

RAND Corporation. 1998. "Preventing Very Low Birthweight Births: A Bundle of Savings." Santa Monica, Calif.: RAND Corporation.

Randall, Bonnie, Susan Bartlett, and Sheela Kennedy. 1998. *Study of WIC Participant and Program Characteristics: 1996.* Cambridge, Mass.: Abt Associates.

Rose, Donald, Jean-Pierre Habicht, and Barbara L. Devaney. 1998. "Household Participation in the Food Stamp and WIC Programs Increases the Nutrient Intakes of Preschool Children." *Journal of Nutrition* 128 (3): 548–55.

Rossi, Peter H. 1998. *Feeding the Poor: Assessing Federal Food Aid.* Washington, D.C.: AEI Press.

Rush, David, Daniel G. Horvitz, W. Burleigh Seaver, Jose M. Alvir, Gail C. Garbowski, Jessica Leighton, Nancy L. Sloan, Sally S. Johnson, Richard A. Kulka, and David S. Shanklin. 1988. "Background and Introduction." *American Journal of Clinical Nutrition* 48 (2): 389–90.

Rush, David, Daniel G. Horvitz, W. Burleigh Seaver, Jessica Leighton, Nancy L. Sloan, Sally S. Johnson, Richard A. Kulka, James W. Devore, Mimi Holt, Judith T. Lynch, Thomas G. Virag, M. Beebe Woodside, and David S. Shanklin. 1988. "Study Methodology and Sample Characteristics in the Longitudinal Study of Pregnant Women, the Study of Children, and the Food Expenditures Study." *American Journal of Clinical Nutrition* 48 (2): 437.

Rush, David, Jessica Leighton, Nancy L. Sloan, Jose M. Alvir, Daniel G. Horvitz, W. Burleigh Seaver, Gail C. Garbowski, Sally S. Johnson, Richard A. Kulka, James W. Devore, Mimi Holt, Judith T. Lynch, Thomas G. Virag, M. Beebe Woodside, and David S. Shanklin. 1988. "Study of Infants and Children." *American Journal of Clinical Nutrition* 48 (2): 484–511.

Rush, David, Nancy L. Sloan, Jessica Leighton, Jose M. Alvir, Daniel G. Horvitz, W. Burleigh Seaver, Gail C. Garbowski, Sally S. Johnson, Richard A. Kulka, Mimi Holt, James W. Devore, Judith T. Lynch, M. Beebe Woodside, and David S. Shanklin. 1988. "Longitudinal Study of Pregnant Women." *American Journal of Clinical Nutrition* 48 (2): 439–83.

Schiller, Janet T., and Mary Kay Fox. 1999. "Nutrition Education: Current Issues and Opportunities: A Synthesis of Recent Research." Presentation at the National Association of WIC Directors annual meeting. New Orleans, La.

Schramm, Wayne F. 1985. "WIC Prenatal Participation and Its Relationship to Newborn Medicaid Costs in Missouri: A Cost/Benefit Analysis." *American Journal of Public Health* 75 (8): 851–57.

———. 1986. "Prenatal Participation in WIC Related to Medicaid Costs for Missouri Newborns: 1982 Update." *Public Health Reports* 101 (6): 614.

Schwartz, J. Brad, David K. Guilkey, John S. Akin, and Barry M. Popkin. 1992. *The WIC Breastfeeding Report: The Relationship of WIC Program Participation to the Initiation and Duration of Breastfeeding.* Alexandria, Va.: U.S. Department of Agriculture, Food and Nutrition Service.

Sherry, Bettylou, Donna Bister, and Ray Yip. 1997. "Continuation of Decline in Prevalence of Anemia in Low-Income Children: The Vermont Experience." *Archives of Pediatrics and Adolescent Medicine* 151 (September): 928–30.

Shiono, Patricia H., and Richard E. Behrman. 1995. "Low Birth Weight: Analysis and Recommendations." *Future of Children* 5 (1): 4–18.

Sigma One Corporation. 2000. "Nutrition Risk and Eligibility for WIC." Durham, N.C.: Sigma One Corporation, November.

Stockbauer, Joseph W. 1987. "WIC Prenatal Participation and Its Relation to Pregnancy Outcomes in Missouri: A Second Look." *American Journal of Public Health* 77 (7): 813–18.

Sullivan, Louis W. 1995. "One for Our Children." *Washington Post,* February 28.

Susser, Mervyn. 1991. "Maternal Weight Gain, Infant Birth Weight, and Diet: Causal Sequences." *American Journal of Clinical Nutrition* 53: 1384–96.

Troiano, Richard P., Katherine M. Flegal, Robert J. Kuczmarski, Stephen M. Campbell, and Clifford L. Johnson. 1995. "Overweight Prevalence and Trends for Children and Adolescents: The National Health and Nutrition Examination Surveys, 1963 to 1991." *Archives of Pediatrics and Adolescent Medicine* 149 (October): 1085–91.

U.S. Department of Agriculture. 1998. "Nutrition Risk Criteria." WIC Policy Memorandum 98-9. June 29.

U.S. Department of Agriculture, Food and Consumer Service. 1997. "WIC: The Special Supplemental Nutrition Program for Women, Infants, and Children." September.

U.S. Department of Agriculture, Food and Nutrition Service, Office of Analysis and Evaluation. 1999. "Special Supplemental Nutrition Program for Women, Infants, and Children (WIC): Eligibility and Coverage Estimates 1997 Update."

———. 2000a. "Fiscal Year 1999 WIC Food Package Costs." November 20.

———. 2000b. *WIC Participant and Program Characteristics Report 1998.* May.

———. 2001. "WIC Categorical Participation." March 20.

U.S. Department of Health and Human Services, Centers for Disease Control, National Center for Health Statistics. 1999. *Health Promotion and Disease Prevention: United States, 1990, Vital and Health Statistics,* series 10, no. 185. Hyattsville, Md.: U.S. Department of Health and Human Services, Centers for Disease Control, National Center for Health Statistics.

U.S. General Accounting Office. 1992. *Early Intervention: Federal Investments Like WIC Can Produce Savings.* GAO/HRD-92-18. Washington, D.C.: Government Printing Office.

———. 1997a. *Head Start: Research Provides Little Information on Impact of Current Program.* GAO/HEHS-97-59. Washington, D.C.: Government Printing Office.

———. 1997b. *A Variety of Practices May Lower the Costs of WIC.* GAO/RCED-97-225. Washington, D.C.: Government Printing Office.

———. 1998. *Information on WIC Sole-Source Rebates and Infant Formula Prices.* GAO/RCED-98-146. Washington, D.C.: Government Printing Office.

———. 1999. *Efforts to Control Fraud and Abuse in the WIC Program Can Be Strengthened.* GAO/RCED-99-224. Washington, D.C.: Government Printing Office.

Watkins, Shirley R. 1998. "Remarks." National Association of WIC Directors Nutrition Education and Breastfeeding Promotion Conference. December 10.

Whaley, Shannon E., and Laurie True. 2000. "California WIC and Proposition 10: Made for Each Other." In *Building Community Systems for Young Children.* Berkeley: University of California, California Policy Research Center.

Yip, Ray. 1989. "The Changing Characteristics of Childhood Iron Nutritional Status in the United States." In L. J. Filer, Jr., ed., *Dietary Iron: Birth to Two Years.* New York: Raven Press.

Yip, Ray, Nancy J. Binkin, Lee Fleshood, and Frederick L. Trowbridge. 1987. "Declining Prevalence of Anemia among Low-Income Children in the United States." *Journal of the American Medical Association* 258 (12): 1610–23.

Index

Index

Urban Institute, 15–16, 28, 63, 76, 111

Voter registration, 15, 65
Vouchers, 11, 14

Waivers, 121, 147 n. 13
Washington, 71
Watkins, Shirley R., 55, 111
Welfare policy, 89
Whaley, Shannon E., 65, 71, 72
White House Conference on Food,
    Nutrition, and Health, 3, 58
Whites, compared with blacks, *see*
    Blacks

WIC program
        characteristics surveys, 119,
    120
        evidence of effects, 97–99,
        115–16
        growth of, 111, 117–18, 124
        overview, 8–9
        and overweight, 61
        proposed reforms and
            variations, 5–7, 62–72,
            99–100, 124
        purpose and scope, 3–4

Yip, Ray, 31, 106

About the Authors
and the Contributors

About the Authors
and the Contributors

Douglas J. Besharov is the Joseph J. and Violet Jacobs Scholar in Social Welfare Studies at the American Enterprise Institute for Public Policy Research, where he is director of the Social and Individual Responsibility Project, and a professor at the University of Maryland School of Public Affairs. He is the author or editor of several books, including *Recognizing Child Abuse: A Guide for the Concerned* (1990), *When Drug Addicts Have Children: Reorienting Child Welfare's Response* (1994), *Enhancing Early Childhood Programs: Burdens and Opportunities* (1996), and *America's Disconnected Youth: Toward a Preventive Strategy* (1999).

Peter Germanis is a research associate at the American Enterprise Institute for Public Policy Research, the assistant director of the University of Maryland's Welfare Reform Academy, and administrator of the Committee to Review Welfare Reform Research. Previously, he was the director of program evaluation at the Office of Family Assistance at the U.S. Department of Health and Human Services and served in the White House under the Reagan and Bush administrations.

Michael J. Brien is assistant professor of economics at the University of Virginia. Previously, he served as a senior economist on the President's Council of Economic Advisers, where he analyzed labor, welfare, and family policy.

Nancy R. Burstein is an economist at Abt Associates, Inc. Over the past twenty years she has directed and implemented a wide variety of policy analyses on income security, employment, health, nutrition, and child development and well-being for state and federal agencies.

Barbara L. Devaney is an economist and senior fellow at Mathematica Policy Research in Princeton, New Jersey. Her research focuses on food assistance and nutrition policy and maternal and child health policy and programs. She has conducted several studies of school nutrition programs, the Food Stamp Program, and the Special Supplemental Nutrition Program for Women, Infants, and Children.

Robert Greenstein is the executive director of the Center on Budget and Policy Priorities. He has served as the administrator of the Food and Nutrition Service at the U.S. Department of Agriculture and was appointed to the Bipartisan Commission on Entitlement and Tax Reform in 1994. In 1996 Mr. Greenstein was awarded a MacArthur Fellowship.

Christopher A. Swann is assistant professor of economics at the State University of New York at Stony Brook. Previously, he taught at the University of Virginia and the University of Michigan and was affiliated with Mathematica Policy Research. Professor Swann's research interests include maternal and child health and welfare policy.